Para ser discípulo y misionero del Señor
Jesús hay que conocer su Palabra es-
crita en los Evangelios.

Con mi bendición,

Francisco

*To be a disciple and missionary of the Lord*
*Jesus we must know his Word written in the Gospels.*
*With my blessing,*
—Francis

# God with Us

The Story of Jesus as Told by Matthew, Mark, Luke, and John

Fundación Ramón Pané

LOYOLA PRESS.
A JESUIT MINISTRY
Chicago

Fundación
Ramón Pané

# LOYOLA PRESS.
## A JESUIT MINISTRY

3441 N. Ashland Avenue
Chicago, Illinois 60657
(800) 621-1008
www.loyolapress.com

The Ramón Pané Foundation takes its name from one of the greatest figures in the evangelization of America. It was founded in 1994 in honor and memory of Ramón Pané, who is considered to be the first missionary to America. It is an international group of Catholics whose mission is to help all the dioceses, Episcopal Conferences and Catholic organizations in educational, missionary and spiritual training. Its main office is in Tegucigalpa, Honduras and it has an office in Miami, USA. For more information about FRP's mission and work, go to www.fundacionpane.org.

Cover art credit: Cover inspired on an original design by Mariana Díaz, from Catamarca, Argentina.

ISBN: 978-0-8294-4807-8
Library of Congress Control Number: 2018948427

Printed in the United States of America.
18 19 20 21 22 23 24 25 26 27 Tshore 10 9 8 7 6 5 4 3 2 1

April 30, 2018

Dear Brothers and Sisters in Christ,

In the Gospel of John, we hear the story of some people who came to the Apostle Philip and they asked him, "We wish to see Jesus!"

We all need to see Jesus. Because only when we come to meet Jesus and know his love, does our life truly begin. Only Jesus can show us the face of the Father.

Our encounter with Jesus begins in the pages of the Gospels. In these pages we meet the Son of the living God. And by listening to his words and reflecting on his example, we come to know that God is with us.

Pope Francis says we should all carry a small copy of the Gospels that can fit in our pockets and we should pull it out and read it whenever we can. We should read a passage every day from the Gospel, the Pope tells us, because it is the only way we can get to know Jesus.

*God With Us* is a unique book that can help us in our search to see Jesus and to know him. This book draws from the stories of the four Gospels and arranges them to form a single, unified narrative, a kind of biography, in which we encounter Jesus Christ, who is *Emmauel*, God with us.

This book also provides questions for reflection and meditation that invite us to read this story prayerfully and personally, in the spirit of the ancient technique of *lectio divina* or sacred reading.

If prayer is conversation, then we need to listen to God as much as we talk to him. "When you read the Bible, God speaks to you," St. Augustine said. "When you pray, you speak to God." We should never read the life of Jesus as students gathering information to prepare for a test. Instead, we should read as friends who want to know everything we can about the One we love—the details of his life; what he is saying and thinking; how he responds to different situations in his life; his attitudes and feelings.

When we read the Gospels daily with prayer, our lives become a journey we are making with Jesus, a pilgrimage of the heart. The more we pray with the Gospels, the more we will have "the mind of Christ"—his thoughts and feelings, seeing reality through his eyes. The more we pray with the Gospels, the more we will feel Christ's call to change the world—to shape society and history according to God's loving plan.

So, I pray that *God With Us* will help you to learn to love spending time with Jesus in the reading of sacred Scripture!

There is a beautiful description of how Blessed Virgin Mary reflected on what she experienced: "But Mary kept all these things, pondering them in her heart." This is a lesson for us. We need to keep Jesus close to our heart—his words, his actions, the scenes from his life. We need to ponder them and pray about them. Just like Mary did.

May our Blessed Mother Mary accompany all of us as we come to the pages of the Gospels, seeking to see Jesus.

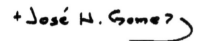

Most Reverend Jose H. Gomez
Archbishop of Los Angeles

Dearest Brothers and Sisters:

The mission and identity of the Church is to evangelize. That is, bring the Good News of the Gospel of our Lord Jesus Christ to all peoples without distinction. When we get started in the project of the Church, we come closer to holiness. The Saints are those who assume the life of Christ as their own. Therefore, it is necessary that we truly get to know the life of Christ in order to follow Him. With this purpose, in his recent Apostolic Exhortation, Pope Francis lets us know the following:

> 19. *A Christian cannot think of his or her mission on earth without seeing it as a path of holiness, for "this is the will of God, your sanctification." Each saint is a mission, planned by the Father to reflect and embody, at a specific moment in history, a certain aspect of the Gospel.*

> 20. *That mission has its fullest meaning in Christ, and can only be understood through him. At its core, holiness is experiencing, in union with Christ, the mysteries of his life. It consists in uniting ourselves to the Lord's death and resurrection in a unique and personal way, constantly dying and rising anew with him. But it can also entail reproducing in our own lives various aspects of Jesus' earthly life: his hidden life, his life in community, his closeness to the outcast, his poverty and other ways in which he showed his self-sacrificing love. The contemplation of these mysteries, as Saint Ignatius of Loyola pointed out, leads us to incarnate them in our choices and attitudes. Because "everything in Jesus' life was a sign of his mystery," "Christ's whole life is a revelation of the Father," "Christ's whole life is a mystery of redemption," "Christ's whole life is a mystery of recapitulation," "Christ enables us to live in him all that he himself lived, and he lives it in us."* (Gaudete et Exsultate 19–20)

I have the pleasure of presenting this work called GOD WITH US, which was put together with great care by the Fundación Ramón Pané, to help its readers know the life of Jesus as written directly by Matthew, Mark, Luke and John. The texts were ordered in a harmonious and chronological format in order to help the readers to truly "follow Christ," because in following Christ we can achieve holiness. At the end of each chapter some questions were added using the method of *lectio divina* to help the reader reflect along this path of holiness. Pope Francis, who dedicated a "Chirograph," or excerpt in his own handwriting, for this book invites us to be disciples as well as missionaries in this work. In *Gaudete et Exsultate* he also tells us:

> "Each in his or her own way" the Council says. We should not grow discouraged before examples of holiness that appear unattainable. There are some testimonies that may prove helpful and inspiring, but that we are not meant to copy, for that could even lead us astray from the one specific path that the Lord has in mind for us. The important thing is that each believer discern his or her own path, that they bring out the very best of themselves, the most personal gifts that God has placed in their hearts (cf. 1 Cor 12:7), rather than hopelessly trying to imitate something not meant for them. We are all called to be witnesses, but there are many actual ways of bearing witness. (Gaudete et Exsultate 11).

This work also can be used as an evangelizing tool, especially by those that are first getting to know Christ. We wish it to be used especially by young people that have taken on the mission of evangelizing their peers within their social circles.

I too want to impart my blessing to those who read the Gospel and have a desire to become announcers of the Good News.

Given in Miami, April 16th, 2018

Archbishop Thomas Wenski
Archbishop of Miami

Fundación
Ramón Pané

My life is permanent travel. God has blessed me with knowing many places in the world, especially as a missionary and evangelist. But the greatest benefit is not all the many landscapes, which undoubtedly speak of the Creator, it is the people. Meeting people from different cultures, ages, social situations, and very different ways of thinking helps me grow in this process called the Christian life.

As a disciple and missionary evangelist, I seriously wonder if we are doing as Jesus asked: "Go . . . to all peoples everywhere and make them my disciples" (Matthew 28:19). The emphasis is on the imperative "go," and I ask myself, *What have we done as disciples and missionaries with this mandate?* Maybe there is enthusiasm in many places, but I still ask myself, *Am I effective in reaching beyond those who participate in our church groups?* The *lectio divina* exercises at the end of each chapter of this book aim to reinforce our Christian vocation as disciples who become missionaries.

The Ramón Pané Foundation is very proud to put in your hands this tool that will be useful for those who know Jesus only from what others say but have not read the Gospels themselves. It is the complete story from the Gospels told chronologically. To facilitate reading, the chapter and verse numbers were eliminated; but the reference for each Scripture selection is put in parentheses for anyone interested in looking for it in the Bible.

We encourage you to become a disciple transformed into a missionary who distributes this simple tool to help many come to know Jesus from the original writings of the New Testament presented in a fresh, new, and concise way.

Courage in your walk!

Bro. Ricardo Grzona, FRP
Director General
Fraternity of Ramón Pané

# Contents

# Introduction

Many people have questions about Jesus. Most people don't know much about him. They might know only what they have heard from others, but some want to find out more. They wonder if what Christians say about him is true. Can he really bring them peace? Can he bring them closer to God?

Jesus Christ was a Jew born in a small village two thousand years ago. He was a carpenter until he was about thirty years old. Then he became a teacher and healer. He traveled less than one hundred miles from his home, and his mission work lasted no more than three years. He preached about God's love and performed many miracles. He attracted a large group of followers. But the religious leaders were afraid of him, so they arrested him and, by convincing Roman authorities that Jesus was a political threat, got him executed through crucifixion.

His followers claimed that he came back to life and returned to heaven. They believed in Jesus, even though many were put in jail or killed for following him. They became known as Christians, and they spread his message throughout the world.

## Why is Jesus so important?

Jesus Christ has affected history more than any other person. What he did changed the world forever. His followers are members of the world's largest religion—there are now more than two billion Christians around the world.

Jesus had a very important message. He talked about God and about life after death. He made some amazing claims about himself. Jesus said, "I have come down from heaven to do not my own will but the will of him who sent me" because "God loved the world so much that he gave his only Son, so that everyone who believes in him may not die but have eternal life."

Many people have believed in Jesus and found his promises to be true. He has brought faith, hope, and purpose to millions of people. Some people don't believe in Jesus Christ or try to live by his teachings, but they may call themselves Christians anyway. Millions of others say that they have come to know Jesus as a real friend. And he changed their lives.

Jesus preached the Good News about God's love for everyone. Yet some people did not believe his message. Jesus warned them. He said, "The teaching you have heard is not mine, but comes from the Father who sent me" and "Those who reject me, who do not accept my message, have one who will judge them. The words I have spoken will be their judge on the last day."

## How do we know about Jesus?

Accounts of Jesus' life were written not long after he died. They are called Gospels (*gospel* means "good news"). These Gospel accounts became part of the Bible that we have today.

Some other Jewish and Roman writers also mention Jesus. Most history scholars today agree that Jesus really did live two thousand years ago.

There are four Gospel accounts in the Bible: these are the Gospels of Matthew, Mark, Luke, and John. The Gospel accounts came from reports by Jesus' followers and by others who knew him.

Jesus chose twelve of his many followers to travel with him, and he called that small group his disciples. They gave personal reports about the things that Jesus said and did.

Matthew was one of the disciples. Before he met Jesus, he collected taxes for the Romans. Matthew's Gospel was meant for Jewish people. It explains how the Jewish Scriptures told about who Jesus really is. His Gospel connects the Old and New Testaments of the Bible.

Mark was a young man who followed Jesus. He was not one of the disciples, but he helped Simon Peter, who was one of the disciples closest to Jesus.

The first Christians met in Mark's mother's house for prayer. His Gospel is a short history of the life and message of Jesus.

Luke was a doctor who knew the disciples. Luke may have learned from Jesus' mother, Mary, many of the things he wrote. Luke said, "Because I have carefully studied all these matters from their beginning, I thought it would be good to write an orderly account for you." Luke also wrote the book of Acts, which describes how the Christian church began.

John was another of the disciples who was a fisherman before he met Jesus. Like Matthew, John traveled with Jesus and saw the things that Jesus did. John's Gospel is about who Jesus really is and why he came. It explains that Jesus is God who became a human being to show us what God is like and to die for our sins.

Bible scholars think that Mark's Gospel was the earliest of the four—written in about AD 70. Matthew and Luke used most of Mark's Gospel in their own accounts. They also used other writings that scholars believe came from a common source.

The Gospels of Matthew, Mark, and Luke are similar to each other, but John's Gospel is different. It contains many details about Jesus that are not found in the other Gospels. His Gospel was written last, around AD 90.

Before the four Gospels were written, the stories about Jesus were handed down by word of mouth. Most people were not able to read at the time of Jesus, so they remembered the sermons of well-known preachers and passed them on. The reports of what Jesus said and what he did were told over and over again.

These reports were included in the Gospels. Luke stated, "Many people have done their best to write a report of the things that have taken place among us. They wrote what we have been told by those who saw these things from the beginning and who proclaimed the message." Many of those people were still alive when the Gospels were written.

The Gospels were collected together with other writings of the early church. This collection is known as the New Testament of the Bible. It is all about the life and message of Jesus Christ. The Old Testament contains the Hebrew Scriptures, what we sometimes refer to as the Jewish Bible.

The Christian church carefully copied and saved the New Testament. We have more copies of the New Testament sources than of any other writings from that time in history.

Jesus and his disciples spoke Aramaic, the language of the Jewish people. But the Gospel writers wrote in Greek, which was a common language of the Roman Empire.

The first English translation of the Greek New Testament was printed in the sixteenth century. The translation was brought up to date when older copies of the New Testament were found. Bible translations are revised from time to time as scholars study the original sources and changes in language.

There are now many different translations of the Bible. Some are word-for-word translations; others are more like thought-for-thought translations. Some Bibles use elegant, old-fashioned language; other Bibles use modern, everyday language.

This book uses the *Good News Translation* (GNT) of the Bible. It is a clear, modern translation that is faithful to the original texts. The Catholic edition includes several deuterocanonical books before the New Testament. Because it is written in everyday language, the Good News Bible has proved to be popular with young people.

### What is this book?

This book selects verses from the Gospels of Matthew, Mark, Luke, and John and weaves them into a single story. It makes it easy to read one chronological account of the life and message of Jesus Christ in a book that is similar to a biography but uses only Scriptures from the Bible. The Scriptures used to tell the story of Jesus are indicated by parentheses at the end of each selection.

None of the four Gospels alone gives a complete picture of Jesus' life, because each Gospel writer chose to highlight different things. The details and order of the events are sometimes different. The purpose of the story was more important than the details of how, where, and when they happened.

The Gospel writers sometimes wrote about similar things happening at a different time or place. Scholars do not always agree on whether these were different events or not. It is likely that Jesus proclaimed the same message on more than one occasion.

Putting this story together required many decisions. Sometimes, when details in the Gospels differ, the text found in more than one Gospel was chosen. Otherwise, the Gospel was selected that best helps you follow the story.

You will notice that, in a few cases, we use text from the Acts of the Apostles. Although technically not a Gospel, "The Acts of the Apostles is a continuation of the Gospel according to Luke. Its chief purpose is to tell how Jesus' early followers, led by the Holy Spirit, spread the Good News about him" (Introduction to The Acts of the Apostles, *Good News Bible*).

At the end of the book, there is a list of Bible references for events in the life of Jesus. You can use this list to find and compare each of the Gospel accounts. There is also a glossary that provides information about the people and customs in the story for readers who are new to the Bible. At the end of each chapter, there are reflections concerning vocation (your calling from God, or purpose in life), discipleship, and mission. Discussion questions are also included in case you want to go deeper.

This book is by no means intended to replace the Bible. It was written to bring the Good News of what Jesus said and did to those who otherwise might not know it. We hope you will read the message of Jesus, understand it, and be inspired to follow Jesus' teachings and example.

# 1

# God Reaches Out

In the beginning the Word already existed; the Word was with God, and the Word was God. From the very beginning the Word was with God. Through him God made all things; not one thing in all creation was made without him.

The Word was the source of life, and this life brought light to people. The light shines in the darkness, and the darkness has never put it out. (John 1:1–5) This was the real light—the light that comes into the world and shines on all people.

The Word was in the world, and though God made the world through him, yet the world did not recognize him. He came to his own country, but his own people did not receive him. Some, however, did receive him and believed in him; so he gave them the right to become God's children. They did not become God's children by natural means, that is, by being born as the children of a human father; God himself was their Father.

The Word became a human being and, full of grace and truth, lived among us. We saw his glory, the glory which he received as the Father's only Son. (John 1:9–14) Out of the fullness of his grace he has blessed us all, giving us one blessing after another.

God gave the Law through Moses, but grace and truth came through Jesus Christ. No one has ever seen God. The only Son, who is the same as God and is at the Father's side, he has made him known. (John 1:16–18)

Dear Theophilus: Many people have done their best to write a report of the things that have taken place among us. They wrote what we have been told by those who saw these things from the beginning and who proclaimed the message. And so, Your Excellency, because I have carefully studied all these matters from their beginning, I [Luke] thought it would be good to write an orderly account for you. I do this so that you will know the full truth about everything which you have been taught.

During the time when Herod was king of Judea, there was a priest named Zechariah, who belonged to the priestly order of Abijah. His wife's name was Elizabeth; she also belonged to a priestly family. They both lived good lives in God's sight and obeyed fully all the Lord's laws and commands. They had no children because Elizabeth could not have any, and she and Zechariah were both very old.

One day Zechariah was doing his work as a priest in the Temple, taking his turn in the daily service. According to the custom followed by the priests, he was chosen by lot to burn incense on the altar. So he went into the Temple of the Lord, while the crowd of people outside prayed during the hour when the incense was burned.

Suddenly, an angel of the Lord appeared to him, standing at the right side of the altar where the incense was burned. When Zechariah saw him, he was alarmed and felt afraid. But the angel said to him, "Don't be afraid, Zechariah! God has heard your prayer, and your wife Elizabeth will bear you a son. You are to name him John. How glad and happy you will be, and how happy many others will be when he is born!

"John will be great in the Lord's sight. He must not drink any wine or strong drink. From his very birth he will be filled with the Holy Spirit, and he will bring back many of the people of Israel to the Lord their God. He will go ahead of the Lord, strong and mighty like the prophet Elijah. He will bring fathers and children together again; he will turn disobedient people back to the way of thinking of the righteous; he will get the Lord's people ready for him."

Zechariah said to the angel, "How shall I know if this is so? I am an old man, and my wife is old also."

"I am Gabriel," the angel answered. "I stand in the presence of God, who sent me to speak to you and tell you this good news. But you have not believed my message, which will come true at the right time. Because you have not believed, you will be unable to speak; you will remain silent until the day my promise to you comes true."

In the meantime the people were waiting for Zechariah and wondering why he was spending such a long time in the Temple. When he came out, he could not speak to them, and so they knew that he had seen a vision in the Temple. Unable to say a word, he made signs to them with his hands.

When his period of service in the Temple was over, Zechariah went back home. Some time later his wife Elizabeth became pregnant and did not leave the house for five months. "Now at last the Lord has helped me," she said. "He has taken away my public disgrace!"

In the sixth month of Elizabeth's pregnancy God sent the angel Gabriel to a town in Galilee named Nazareth. He had a message for a young woman promised in marriage to a man named Joseph, who was a descendant of King David. Her name was Mary. The angel came to her and said, "Peace be with you! The Lord is with you and has greatly blessed you!"

Mary was deeply troubled by the angel's message, and she wondered what his words meant. The angel said to her, "Don't be afraid, Mary; God has been gracious to you. You will become pregnant and give birth to a son, and you will name him Jesus. He will be great and will be called the Son of the Most High God. The Lord God will make him a king, as his ancestor David was, and he will be the king of the descendants of Jacob forever; his kingdom will never end!"

Mary said to the angel, "I am a virgin. How, then, can this be?"

The angel answered, "The Holy Spirit will come on you, and God's power will rest upon you. For this reason the holy child will be called the Son of God. Remember your relative Elizabeth. It is said that she cannot have children, but she herself is now six months pregnant, even though she is very old. For there is nothing that God cannot do."

"I am the Lord's servant," said Mary; "may it happen to me as you have said." And the angel left her.

Soon afterward Mary got ready and hurried off to a town in the hill country of Judea. She went into Zechariah's house and greeted Elizabeth. When Elizabeth heard Mary's greeting, the baby moved within her. Elizabeth was filled with the Holy Spirit and said in a loud voice, "You are the most blessed of all women, and blessed is the child you will bear! Why should this great thing happen to me, that my Lord's mother comes to visit me? For as soon as I heard your greeting, the baby within me jumped with gladness. How happy you are to believe that the Lord's message to you will come true!"

Mary said, "My heart praises the Lord; my soul is glad because of God my Savior, for he has remembered me, his lowly servant! From now on all people will call me happy, because of the great things the Mighty God has done for me.

"His name is holy; from one generation to another he shows mercy to those who honor him. He has stretched out his mighty arm and scattered the proud with all their plans. He has brought down mighty kings from their thrones, and lifted up the lowly. He has filled the hungry with good things, and sent the rich away with empty hands.

"He has kept the promise he made to our ancestors, and has come to the help of his servant Israel. He has remembered to show mercy to Abraham and to all his descendants forever!"

Mary stayed about three months with Elizabeth and then went back home.

The time came for Elizabeth to have her baby, and she gave birth to a son. Her neighbors and relatives heard how wonderfully good the Lord had been to her, and they all rejoiced with her.

When the baby was a week old, they came to circumcise him, and they were going to name him Zechariah, after his father. But his mother said, "No! His name is to be John."

They said to her, "But you don't have any relative with that name!" Then they made signs to his father, asking him what name he would like the boy to have.

Zechariah asked for a writing pad and wrote, "His name is John." How surprised they all were! At that moment Zechariah was able to speak again, and he started praising God. The neighbors were all filled with fear, and the news about these things spread through all the hill country of Judea. Everyone who heard of it thought about it and asked, "What is this child going to be?" For it was plain that the Lord's power was upon him.

John's father Zechariah was filled with the Holy Spirit, and he spoke God's message: "Let us praise the Lord, the God of Israel! He has come to the help of his people and has set them free. He has provided for us a mighty Savior, a descendant of his servant David. He promised through his holy prophets long ago that he would save us from our enemies, from the power of all those who hate us. He said he would show mercy to our ancestors and remember his sacred covenant. With a solemn oath to our ancestor Abraham he promised to rescue us from our enemies and allow us to serve him without fear, so that we might be holy and righteous before him all the days of our life.

"You, my child, will be called a prophet of the Most High God. You will go ahead of the Lord to prepare his road for him, to tell his people that they will be saved by having their sins forgiven. Our God is merciful and tender. He will cause the bright dawn of salvation to rise on us, and to shine from heaven on all those who live in the dark shadow of death, to guide our steps into the path of peace."

The child grew and developed in body and spirit. He lived in the desert until the day when he appeared publicly to the people of Israel. (Luke 1:1–80)

# Reflections and Questions

## About the Reading

Notice that in this chapter we come across two announcements: one to Zechariah and the other to Mary. He is an elderly man who can't have children; she is young and full of life, and her decision will bring life—with a capital *L*—to humanity. God sent his messenger to both of them and gave each a mission.

As with any mission, whoever is tasked with it will be fearful. But believing that everything is possible for God leads these people to say yes, even if they don't understand how everything will come about.

Mary immediately decided to serve, to go see Elizabeth and perhaps help her. Her reunion with Elizabeth takes place in a joyful setting, and it is there that "my Lord's mother" (as Elizabeth called Mary) tells the story of salvation—that is, God's intervention for his people, which now reaches its high point.

## Let's Meditate

God has a mission for each of us.

- Have you considered that, like Zechariah and Mary, you also are being called by God to a certain mission or task?
- How does this reading affect your thinking about your vocation, or calling, in life?
- What does God want you to do in his name?
- Are you also afraid that God will call you to something for which you don't feel ready? If so, how can this reading inspire you to respond?
- Identify aspects of Mary and Zechariah's callings that can help you follow your own life and vocation.

## Ask God

Take some time for quiet reflection. In your own words, ask God to show you, through this Gospel reading, a clear path to the calling he has revealed to you.

**Think about the Main Idea**

Look for the phrase in the reading that most catches your attention, and repeat it to yourself several times. You might also write it in a journal so that you can revisit it and think about it again.

**Create an Action Plan**

Reading the Bible and praying with it can move us to change.

- How can this reading help you understand your calling better?
- What concrete action can you take to bring your prayer and meditation into daily life?

**Discussion Questions**

1. The story of Jesus begins with some words such as *life, light, children of God, glory*, and *grace*. Which phrase stands out the most to you? What do you find interesting about it?
2. If you were Mary, what would you be feeling and thinking about your pregnancy? In what ways would you feel blessed? How might others react to your situation?
3. Zechariah foretold that his son, John, would prepare the way for the Lord by telling people how they could find salvation. What might lead someone to feel that he or she needs salvation from something? Reflect on your own life; what do *you* need salvation from?

# 2

# A Special Birth

This was how the birth of Jesus Christ took place. His mother Mary was engaged to Joseph, but before they were married, she found out that she was going to have a baby by the Holy Spirit. Joseph was a man who always did what was right, but he did not want to disgrace Mary publicly; so he made plans to break the engagement privately.

While he was thinking about this, an angel of the Lord appeared to him in a dream and said, "Joseph, descendant of David, do not be afraid to take Mary to be your wife. For it is by the Holy Spirit that she has conceived. She will have a son, and you will name him Jesus—because he will save his people from their sins."

Now all this happened in order to make come true what the Lord had said through the prophet, "A virgin will become pregnant and have a son, and he will be called Immanuel" (which means, "God is with us").

So when Joseph woke up, he married Mary, as the angel of the Lord had told him to. But he had no sexual relations with her before she gave birth to her son. And Joseph named him Jesus. (Matthew 1:18–25)

Jesus was born in the town of Bethlehem in Judea, during the time when Herod was king. (Matthew 2:1) At that time Emperor Augustus ordered a census to be taken throughout the Roman Empire. When this first census took place, Quirinius was the governor of Syria. Everyone, then, went to register himself, each to his own hometown.

Joseph went from the town of Nazareth in Galilee to the town of Bethlehem in Judea, the birthplace of King David. Joseph went there because he was a descendant of David. He went to register with Mary, who was promised in marriage to him. She was pregnant, and while they were in Bethlehem, the time came for her to have her baby. She gave birth to her first son, wrapped him in cloths and laid him in a manger—because there was no room for them to stay in the inn.

There were some shepherds in that part of the country who were spending the night in the fields, taking care of their flocks. An angel of the Lord appeared to them, and the glory of the Lord shone over them. They were terribly afraid, but the angel said to them, "Don't be afraid! I am here with good news for you, which will bring great joy to all the people. This very day in David's town your Savior was born—Christ the Lord! And this is what will prove it to you: you will find a baby wrapped in cloths and lying in a manger."

Suddenly a great army of heaven's angels appeared with the angel, singing praises to God: "Glory to God in the highest heaven, and peace on earth to those with whom he is pleased!"

When the angels went away from them back into heaven, the shepherds said to one another, "Let's go to Bethlehem and see this thing that has happened, which the Lord has told us."

So they hurried off and found Mary and Joseph and saw the baby lying in the manger. When the shepherds saw him, they told them what the angel had said about the child. All who heard it were amazed at what the shepherds said. Mary remembered all these things and thought deeply about them.

The shepherds went back, singing praises to God for all they had heard and seen; it had been just as the angel had told them.

A week later, when the time came for the baby to be circumcised, he was named Jesus, the name which the angel had given him before he had been conceived.

Then the time came for Joseph and Mary to perform the ceremony of purification, as the Law of Moses commanded. So they took the child to Jerusalem to present him to the Lord, as it is written in the law of the Lord: "Every first-born male is to be dedicated to the Lord." They also went to offer a sacrifice of a pair of doves or two young pigeons, as required by the law of the Lord.

At that time there was a man named Simeon living in Jerusalem. He was a good, God-fearing man and was waiting for Israel to be saved. The Holy Spirit was with him and had assured him that he would not die before he had seen the Lord's promised Messiah.

Led by the Spirit, Simeon went into the Temple. When the parents brought the child Jesus into the Temple to do for him what the Law required, Simeon took the child in his arms and gave thanks to God: "Now, Lord, you have kept your promise, and you may let your servant go in peace. With my own eyes I have seen your salvation, which you have prepared in the presence of all peoples: A light to reveal your will to the Gentiles and bring glory to your people Israel."

The child's father and mother were amazed at the things Simeon said about him. Simeon blessed them and said to Mary, his mother, "This child is chosen by God for the destruction and the salvation of many in Israel. He will be a sign from God which many people will speak against and so reveal their secret thoughts. And sorrow, like a sharp sword, will break your own heart."

There was a very old prophet, a widow named Anna, daughter of Phanuel of the tribe of Asher. She had been married for only seven years and was now eighty-four years old. She never left the Temple; day and night she worshiped God, fasting and praying. That very same hour she arrived and gave thanks to God and spoke about the child to all who were waiting for God to set Jerusalem free. (Luke 2:1–38)

Soon afterward, some men who studied the stars came from the East to Jerusalem and asked, "Where is the baby born to be the king of the Jews? We saw his star when it came up in the east, and we have come to worship him."

When King Herod heard about this, he was very upset, and so was everyone else in Jerusalem. He called together all the chief priests and the teachers of the Law and asked them, "Where will the Messiah be born?"

"In the town of Bethlehem in Judea," they answered. "For this is what the prophet wrote: 'Bethlehem in the land of Judah, you are by no means the least of the leading cities of Judah; for from you will come a leader who will guide my people Israel.'"

So Herod called the visitors from the East to a secret meeting and found out from them the exact time the star had appeared. Then he sent them to Bethlehem with these instructions: "Go and make a careful search for the child; and when you find him, let me know, so that I too may go and worship him."

And so they left, and on their way they saw the same star they had seen in the East. When they saw it, how happy they were, what joy was theirs! It went ahead of them until it stopped over the place where the child was. They went into the house, and when they saw the child with his mother Mary, they knelt down and worshiped him. They brought out their gifts of gold, frankincense, and myrrh, and presented them to him.

Then they returned to their country by another road, since God had warned them in a dream not to go back to Herod.

After they had left, an angel of the Lord appeared in a dream to Joseph and said, "Herod will be looking for the child in order to kill him. So get up, take the child and his mother and escape to Egypt, and stay there until I tell you to leave."

Joseph got up, took the child and his mother, and left during the night for Egypt, where he stayed until Herod died. This was done to make come true what the Lord had said through the prophet, "I called my Son out of Egypt."

When Herod realized that the visitors from the East had tricked him, he was furious. He gave orders to kill all the boys in Bethlehem and its neighborhood who were two years old and younger—this was done in accordance with what he had learned from the visitors about the time when the star had appeared.

In this way what the prophet Jeremiah had said came true: "A sound is heard in Ramah, the sound of bitter weeping. Rachel is crying for her children; she refuses to be comforted, for they are dead."

After Herod died, an angel of the Lord appeared in a dream to Joseph in Egypt and said, "Get up, take the child and his mother, and go back to the land of Israel, because those who tried to kill the child are dead." So Joseph got up, took the child and his mother, and went back to Israel. But when Joseph heard that Archelaus had succeeded his father Herod as king of Judea, he was afraid to go there. He was given more instructions in a dream, so he went to the province of Galilee and made his home in a town named Nazareth. So what the prophets had said came true: "He will be called a Nazarene." (Matthew 2:1–23)

The child grew and became strong; he was full of wisdom, and God's blessings were upon him.

Every year the parents of Jesus went to Jerusalem for the Passover Festival. When Jesus was twelve years old, they went to the festival as usual. When the festival was over, they started back home, but the boy Jesus stayed in Jerusalem. His parents did not know this; they thought that he was with the group, so they traveled a whole day and then started looking for him among their relatives and friends. They did not find him, so they went back to Jerusalem looking for him.

On the third day they found him in the Temple, sitting with the Jewish teachers, listening to them and asking questions. All who heard him were amazed at his intelligent answers. His parents were astonished when they saw him, and his mother said to him, "Son, why have you done this to us? Your father and I have been terribly worried trying to find you."

He answered them, "Why did you have to look for me? Didn't you know that I had to be in my Father's house?" But they did not understand his answer. So Jesus went back with them to Nazareth, where he was obedient to them. And his mother treasured all these things in her heart.

Jesus grew both in body and in wisdom, gaining favor with God and people. (Luke 2:40–52)

# Reflections and Questions

## About the Reading

On two separate occasions, Joseph received warnings in dreams: to accept Jesus and his mother, and to save them from death by fleeing to Egypt. His purpose in life was to watch over Jesus. Joseph believed, so he acted on faith. His decision could not have been easy, but here we see him following the Lord's will at every turn.

Notice in this reading all the characters who seek Jesus in order to recognize and worship him: the shepherds, Simeon, Anna, and the visitors from the East. Each one was called in a different way to seek the Lord, because every person has a different story.

Finally we come across Jesus in the temple, speaking to the Jewish teachers. From a very young age, Jesus understood his vocation.

## Let's Meditate

God has a mission for each of us.

- Are you able to listen to the voice of God and his messengers?
- How can you live out Jesus' message of salvation today?
- Accepting a calling involves leaving your comfort zone. Are you willing to do this?
- What do you think God has planned for you? Are you ready to follow Jesus?
- The people in these Scriptures publicly acknowledged the Lord. One of God's first callings for us is to publicly acknowledge Jesus as Lord and Savior. Is there anything that stops you from doing this publicly?

## Ask God

Take some time for quiet reflection. In your own words, ask God to show you, through this Gospel reading, a clear path to the calling he has revealed to you.

**Think about the Main Idea**

Look for the phrase in the reading that most catches your attention, and repeat it to yourself several times. You might also write it in a journal so that you can revisit it and think about it again.

**Create an Action Plan**

Reading the Bible and praying with it can move us to change.

- How can this reading help you understand your calling better?
- What concrete action can you take to bring your prayer and meditation into daily life?

**Discussion Questions**

1. Jesus' birth was quite different from what might be expected for the Savior of the world. Instead of being surrounded by royalty and rituals, he was surrounded by animals, along with their sounds and smells. What do the circumstances of Jesus' birth say about God?
2. Joseph and Mary were in a situation that likely felt both wonderful and terrifying. When have you experienced a situation that felt both wonderful and terrifying? What fears or hopes crossed your mind?
3. Isaiah prophesies that a virgin will miraculously have a baby and that he will be called Emmanuel, which means "God is with us." Have you ever felt that God was with you? When? In what area of your life are you eager to have God's presence?

# 3

# **Preparing the Way**

God sent his messenger, a man named John, who came to tell people about the light, so that all should hear the message and believe. He himself was not the light; he came to tell about the light. (John 1:6–8)

It was the fifteenth year of the rule of Emperor Tiberius; Pontius Pilate was governor of Judea, Herod was ruler of Galilee, and his brother Philip was ruler of the territory of Iturea and Trachonitis; Lysanias was ruler of Abilene, and Annas and Caiaphas were High Priests.

At that time the word of God came to John son of Zechariah in the desert. So John went throughout the whole territory of the Jordan River, preaching, "Turn away from your sins and be baptized, and God will forgive your sins." (Luke 3:1–3) "Turn away from your sins," he said, "because the Kingdom of heaven is near!"

John was the man the prophet Isaiah was talking about when he said, "Someone is shouting in the desert, 'Prepare a road for the Lord; make a straight path for him to travel!'"

John's clothes were made of camel's hair; he wore a leather belt around his waist, and his food was locusts and wild honey. People came to him from Jerusalem, from the whole province of Judea, and from all over the country near the Jordan River. They confessed their sins, and he baptized them in the Jordan.

When John saw many Pharisees and Sadducees coming to him to be baptized, he said to them, "You snakes—who told you that you could escape from the punishment God is about to send? Do those things that will show that you have turned from your sins. And don't think you can escape punishment by saying that Abraham is your ancestor. I tell you that God can take these rocks and make descendants for Abraham! The ax is ready to cut down the trees at the roots; every tree that does not bear good fruit will be cut down and thrown in the fire. (Matthew 3:2–10)

The people asked him, "What are we to do, then?"

He answered, "Whoever has two shirts must give one to the man who has none, and whoever has food must share it."

Some tax collectors came to be baptized, and they asked him, "Teacher, what are we to do?"

"Don't collect more than is legal," he told them.

Some soldiers also asked him, "What about us? What are we to do?"

He said to them, "Don't take money from anyone by force or accuse anyone falsely. Be content with your pay."

People's hopes began to rise, and they began to wonder whether John perhaps might be the Messiah. So John said to all of them, "I baptize you with water, but someone is coming who is much greater than I am. I am not good enough even to untie his sandals. He will baptize you with the Holy Spirit and fire. He has his winnowing shovel with him, to thresh out all the grain and gather the wheat into his barn; but he will burn the chaff in a fire that never goes out."

In many different ways John preached the Good News to the people and urged them to change their ways. (Luke 3:10–18)


When Jesus began his work, he was about thirty years old. (Luke 3:23) At that time Jesus arrived from Galilee and came to John at the Jordan to be baptized by him. But John tried to make him change his mind. "I ought to be baptized by you," John said, "and yet you have come to me!"

But Jesus answered him, "Let it be so for now. For in this way we shall do all that God requires."

So John agreed. As soon as Jesus was baptized, he came up out of the water. Then heaven was opened to him, and he saw the Spirit of God coming down like a dove and lighting on him. Then a voice said from heaven, "This is my own dear Son, with whom I am pleased." (Matthew 3:13–17)

Then the Spirit led Jesus into the desert to be tempted by the Devil. After spending forty days and nights without food, Jesus was hungry. Then the Devil came to him and said, "If you are God's Son, order these stones to turn into bread."

Jesus answered, "The scripture says, 'Human beings cannot live on bread alone, but need every word that God speaks.'"

Then the Devil took Jesus to Jerusalem, the Holy City, set him on the highest point of the Temple, and said to him, "If you are God's Son, throw yourself down, for the scripture says, 'God will give orders to his angels about you; they will hold you up with their hands, so that not even your feet will be hurt on the stones.'"

Jesus answered, "But the scripture also says, 'Do not put the Lord your God to the test.'"

Then the Devil took Jesus to a very high mountain and showed him all the kingdoms of the world in all their greatness. "All this I will give you," the Devil said, "if you kneel down and worship me."

Then Jesus answered, "Go away, Satan! The scripture says, 'Worship the Lord your God and serve only him!'"

Then the Devil left Jesus; and angels came and helped him. (Matthew 4:1–11)

The Jewish authorities in Jerusalem sent some priests and Levites to John to ask him, "Who are you?"

John did not refuse to answer, but spoke out openly and clearly, saying: "I am not the Messiah."

"Who are you, then?" they asked. "Are you Elijah?"

"No, I am not," John answered.

"Are you the Prophet?" they asked.

"No," he replied.

"Then tell us who you are," they said. "We have to take an answer back to those who sent us. What do you say about yourself?"

John answered by quoting the prophet Isaiah: "I am 'the voice of someone shouting in the desert: Make a straight path for the Lord to travel!'"

The messengers, who had been sent by the Pharisees, then asked John, "If you are not the Messiah nor Elijah nor the Prophet, why do you baptize?"

John answered, "I baptize with water, but among you stands the one you do not know. He is coming after me, but I am not good enough even to untie his sandals."

All this happened in Bethany on the east side of the Jordan River, where John was baptizing.

The next day John saw Jesus coming to him, and said, "There is the Lamb of God, who takes away the sin of the world! This is the one I was talking about when I said, 'A man is coming after me, but he is greater than I am, because he existed before I was born.' I did not know who he would be, but I came baptizing with water in order to make him known to the people of Israel."

And John gave this testimony: "I saw the Spirit come down like a dove from heaven and stay on him. I still did not know that he was the one, but God, who sent me to baptize with water, had said to me, 'You will see the Spirit come down and stay on a man; he is the one who baptizes with the Holy Spirit.' I have seen it," said John, "and I tell you that he is the Son of God." (John 1:19–34)

# Reflections and Questions

## About the Reading

John the Baptist was not the Light, but he was a witness to the Light. He had decided to dedicate his life to prayer and living in the desert. That's where the Word of God called him to proclaim a message of repentance. Once again, we see God changing human plans. John's vocation of spreading the Good News and denouncing everything that opposes it represents years of prayer, silence, and listening to discern the will of God.

Jesus stood in line with sinners waiting to be baptized. To human eyes, it is unclear why; but the voice of the Father assures us that Jesus is his beloved Son, who did what was right.

Jesus, in preparation for his public mission, goes to the desert, and there he is tempted. The funny thing is that the Devil tempts him by using Scripture, obviously taken way out of context. Jesus responds with Scripture, rightly used. As John the Baptist proclaimed, Jesus is the Lamb of God who takes away the sin of the world. He is the one to follow.

## Let's Meditate

God has a mission for each of us.

- John spent his life in the desert and in prayer. Do you recognize that in order to understand your vocation, you, too, must devote more time listening to God?
- What steps do you take to set aside a special time during the day to devote to prayer?
- Can you identify the obstacles that get in the way of your prayer?
- In your Christian life, how do you proclaim the Kingdom of God and denounce injustice?
- Can you identify the biggest temptations stopping you from carrying out your vocation?
- Can you say, "I am a follower—that is, a true disciple of Jesus"?

## Ask God

Take some time for quiet reflection. In your own words, ask God to show you, through this Gospel reading, a clear path to the calling he has revealed to you.

## Think about the Main Idea

Look for the phrase in the reading that most catches your attention, and repeat it to yourself several times. You might also write it in a journal so that you can revisit it and think about it again.

## Create an Action Plan

Reading the Bible and praying with it can move us to change.

- How can this reading help you understand your calling better?
- What concrete action can you take to bring your prayer and meditation into daily life?

## Discussion Questions

1. As John performed baptisms, he gave some especially harsh warnings to the religious leaders of the day. What was he trying to say to them, and why do you think he was so hard on them?

2. When Jesus is baptized by John, a voice speaks from heaven, "This is my own dear Son, with whom I am pleased." There was nothing Jesus did to earn his heavenly father's love; his heavenly father loved him no matter what. When have you sensed that same unconditional love from God or from someone else?

3. When have you experienced temptations that are tough to resist? How can Jesus' response during his time in the desert guide you when you feel tested?

# 4

# Jesus Starts His Mission

The next day John was standing there again with two of his disciples, when he saw Jesus walking by. "There is the Lamb of God!" he said.

The two disciples heard him say this and went with Jesus. Jesus turned, saw them following him, and asked, "What are you looking for?"

They answered, "Where do you live, Rabbi?" (This word means "Teacher.")

"Come and see," he answered. (It was then about four o'clock in the afternoon.) So they went with him and saw where he lived, and spent the rest of that day with him.

One of them was Andrew, Simon Peter's brother. At once he found his brother Simon and told him, "We have found the Messiah." (This word means "Christ.") Then he took Simon to Jesus.

Jesus looked at him and said, "Your name is Simon son of John, but you will be called Cephas." (This is the same as Peter and means "a rock.")

The next day Jesus decided to go to Galilee. He found Philip and said to him, "Come with me!" (Philip was from Bethsaida, the town where Andrew and Peter lived.) Philip found Nathanael and told him, "We have found the one whom Moses wrote about in the book of the Law and whom the prophets also wrote about. He is Jesus son of Joseph, from Nazareth."

"Can anything good come from Nazareth?" Nathanael asked.

"Come and see," answered Philip.

When Jesus saw Nathanael coming to him, he said about him, "Here is a real Israelite; there is nothing false in him!"

Nathanael asked him, "How do you know me?"

Jesus answered, "I saw you when you were under the fig tree before Philip called you."

"Teacher," answered Nathanael, "you are the Son of God! You are the King of Israel!"

Jesus said, "Do you believe just because I told you I saw you when you were under the fig tree? You will see much greater things than this!" And he said to them, "I am telling you the truth: you will see heaven open and God's angels going up and coming down on the Son of Man." (John 1:35–51)

Two days later there was a wedding in the town of Cana in Galilee. Jesus' mother was there, and Jesus and his disciples had also been invited to the wedding. When the wine had given out, Jesus' mother said to him, "They are out of wine."

"You must not tell me what to do," Jesus replied. "My time has not yet come."

Jesus' mother then told the servants, "Do whatever he tells you."

The Jews have rules about ritual washing, and for this purpose six stone water jars were there, each one large enough to hold between twenty and thirty gallons. Jesus said to the servants, "Fill these jars with water." They filled them to the brim, and then he told them, "Now draw some water out and take it to the man in charge of the feast."

They took him the water, which now had turned into wine, and he tasted it. He did not know where this wine had come from (but, of course, the servants who had drawn out the water knew); so he called the bridegroom and said to him, "Everyone else serves the best wine first, and after the guests have drunk a lot, he serves the ordinary wine. But you have kept the best wine until now!"

Jesus performed this first miracle in Cana in Galilee; there he revealed his glory, and his disciples believed in him. After this, Jesus and his mother, brothers, and disciples went to Capernaum and stayed there a few days. (John 2:1–12)

There was a Jewish leader named Nicodemus, who belonged to the party of the Pharisees. One night he went to Jesus and said to him, "Rabbi, we know that you are a teacher sent by God. No one could perform the miracles you are doing unless God were with him."

Jesus answered, "I am telling you the truth: no one can see the Kingdom of God without being born again."

"How can a grown man be born again?" Nicodemus asked. "He certainly cannot enter his mother's womb and be born a second time!"

"I am telling you the truth," replied Jesus, "that no one can enter the Kingdom of God without being born of water and the Spirit. A person is born physically of human parents, but is born spiritually of the Spirit. Do not be surprised because I tell you that you must all be born again. The wind blows wherever it wishes; you hear the sound it makes, but you do not know where it comes from or where it is going. It is like that with everyone who is born of the Spirit."

"How can this be?" asked Nicodemus.

Jesus answered, "You are a great teacher in Israel, and you don't know this? I am telling you the truth: we speak of what we know and report what we have seen, yet none of you is willing to accept our message. You do not believe me when I tell you about the things of this world; how will you ever believe me, then, when I tell you about the things of heaven? And no one has ever gone up to heaven except the Son of Man, who came down from heaven.

"As Moses lifted up the bronze snake on a pole in the desert, in the same way the Son of Man must be lifted up, so that everyone who believes in him may have eternal life. For God loved the world so much that he gave his only Son, so that everyone who believes in him may not die but have eternal life. For God did not send his Son into the world to be its judge, but to be its savior.

"Those who believe in the Son are not judged; but those who do not believe have already been judged, because they have not believed in God's only Son. This is how the judgment works: the light has come into the world, but people love the darkness rather than the light, because their deeds are evil. Those who do evil things hate the light and will not come to the light, because they do not want their evil deeds to be shown up. But those who do what is true come to the light in order that the light may show that what they did was in obedience to God."

After this, Jesus and his disciples went to the province of Judea, where he spent some time with them and baptized. John also was baptizing in Aenon, not far from Salim, because there was plenty of water in that place. People were going to him, and he was baptizing them. (This was before John had been put in prison.)

Some of John's disciples began arguing with a Jew about the matter of ritual washing. So they went to John and told him, "Teacher, you remember the man who was with you on the east side of the Jordan, the one you spoke about? Well, he is baptizing now, and everyone is going to him!"

John answered, "No one can have anything unless God gives it. You yourselves are my witnesses that I said, 'I am not the Messiah, but I have been sent ahead of him.' The bridegroom is the one to whom the bride belongs; but the bridegroom's friend, who stands by and listens, is glad when he hears the bridegroom's voice. This is how my own happiness is made complete. He must become more important while I become less important.

"He who comes from above is greater than all. He who is from the earth belongs to the earth and speaks about earthly matters, but he who comes from heaven is above all. He tells what he has seen and heard, yet no one accepts his message. But whoever accepts his message confirms by this that God is truthful. The one whom God has sent speaks God's words, because God gives him the fullness of his Spirit. The Father loves his Son and has put everything in his power. Whoever believes in the Son has eternal life; whoever disobeys the Son will not have life, but will remain under God's punishment." (John 3:1–36)

The Pharisees heard that Jesus was winning and baptizing more disciples than John. (Actually, Jesus himself did not baptize anyone; only his disciples did.) So when Jesus heard what was being said, he left Judea and went back to Galilee; on his way there he had to go through Samaria.

In Samaria he came to a town named Sychar, which was not far from the field that Jacob had given to his son Joseph. Jacob's well was there, and Jesus, tired out by the trip, sat down by the well. It was about noon.

A Samaritan woman came to draw some water, and Jesus said to her, "Give me a drink of water." (His disciples had gone into town to buy food.)

The woman answered, "You are a Jew, and I am a Samaritan—so how can you ask me for a drink?" (Jews will not use the same cups and bowls that Samaritans use.)

Jesus answered, "If you only knew what God gives and who it is that is asking you for a drink, you would ask him, and he would give you life-giving water."

"Sir," the woman said, "you don't have a bucket, and the well is deep. Where would you get that life-giving water? It was our ancestor Jacob who gave us this well; he and his children and his flocks all drank from it. You don't claim to be greater than Jacob, do you?"

Jesus answered, "Those who drink this water will get thirsty again, but those who drink the water that I will give them will never be thirsty again. The water that I will give them will become in them a spring which will provide them with life-giving water and give them eternal life."

"Sir," the woman said, "give me that water! Then I will never be thirsty again, nor will I have to come here to draw water."

"Go and call your husband," Jesus told her, "and come back."

"I don't have a husband," she answered.

Jesus replied, "You are right when you say you don't have a husband. You have been married to five men, and the man you live with now is not really your husband. You have told me the truth."

"I see you are a prophet, sir," the woman said. "My Samaritan ancestors worshiped God on this mountain, but you Jews say that Jerusalem is the place where we should worship God."

Jesus said to her, "Believe me, woman, the time will come when people will not worship the Father either on this mountain or in Jerusalem. You Samaritans do not really know whom you worship; but we Jews know whom we worship, because it is from the Jews that salvation comes. But the time is coming and is already here, when by the power of God's Spirit people will worship the Father as he really is, offering him the true worship that he wants. God is Spirit, and only by the power of his Spirit can people worship him as he really is."

The woman said to him, "I know that the Messiah will come, and when he comes, he will tell us everything."

Jesus answered, "I am he, I who am talking with you."

At that moment Jesus' disciples returned, and they were greatly surprised to find him talking with a woman. But none of them said to her, "What do you want?" or asked him, "Why are you talking with her?"

Then the woman left her water jar, went back to the town, and said to the people there, "Come and see the man who told me everything I have ever done. Could he be the Messiah?" So they left the town and went to Jesus.

In the meantime the disciples were begging Jesus, "Teacher, have something to eat!"

But he answered, "I have food to eat that you know nothing about."

So the disciples started asking among themselves, "Could somebody have brought him food?"

"My food," Jesus said to them, "is to obey the will of the one who sent me and to finish the work he gave me to do. You have a saying, 'Four more months and then the harvest.' But I tell you, take a good look at the fields; the crops are now ripe and ready to be harvested! The one who reaps the harvest is being paid and gathers the crops for eternal life; so the one who plants and the one who reaps will be glad together. For the saying is true, 'Someone plants, someone else reaps.' I have sent you to reap a harvest in a field where you did not work; others worked there, and you profit from their work."

Many of the Samaritans in that town believed in Jesus because the woman had said, "He told me everything I have ever done." So when the Samaritans came to him, they begged him to stay with them, and Jesus stayed there two days.

Many more believed because of his message, and they told the woman, "We believe now, not because of what you said, but because we ourselves have heard him, and we know that he really is the Savior of the world."

After spending two days there, Jesus left and went to Galilee. For he himself had said, "Prophets are not respected in their own country." When he arrived in Galilee, the people there welcomed him, because they had gone to the Passover Festival in Jerusalem and had seen everything that he had done during the festival.

Then Jesus went back to Cana in Galilee, where he had turned the water into wine. A government official was there whose son was sick in Capernaum. When he heard that Jesus had come from Judea to Galilee, he went to him and asked him to go to Capernaum and heal his son, who was about to die. Jesus said to him, "None of you will ever believe unless you see miracles and wonders."

"Sir," replied the official, "come with me before my child dies."

Jesus said to him, "Go; your son will live!"

The man believed Jesus' words and went. On his way home his servants met him with the news, "Your boy is going to live!"

He asked them what time it was when his son got better, and they answered, "It was one o'clock yesterday afternoon when the fever left him." Then the father remembered that it was at that very hour when Jesus had told him, "Your son will live." So he and all his family believed.

This was the second miracle that Jesus performed after coming from Judea to Galilee. (John 4:1–54)

# Reflections and Questions

## About the Reading

As you continue reading, you'll understand that Jesus began his mission by calling those he wanted. His first followers left everything to follow him. For some, finding the Messiah means a change of name and vocation—as is the case of Simon, whom Jesus called Peter.

Jesus also participated in the daily life of his people, and he blessed the wedding with new wine.

With Nicodemus, Jesus spoke of a new birth in the Spirit. However, he clarified that we must believe in the Son, who is sent by the Father. Believing is the beginning of a calling to follow the Lord.

Jesus had no problem talking to a woman from Samaria and letting her know that he is the life-giving water and that those who come to him will never thirst again. He knows about human life and its mistakes and sins. Yet he seeks out the woman, speaking to her about redemption for those who are not part of the people of Israel.

This part of the Gospel of John ends with Jesus announcing that the government official's son is healed. Jesus calls us to live a full life, and the signs are there for us to believe.

## Let's Meditate

God has a mission for each of us.

- Do you approach Jesus with the attitude of a follower and ask him, "Where do you live?"
- Do you allow Jesus to tell your personal story and unite it with the great story of salvation?
- If, like Nicodemus, you were to come to Jesus to defend your belief system, how do you think he would respond to you? What do you think he would ask of you?
- Jesus reaches out to you as he did to the Samaritan woman. Cultural and religious differences might have stood in the way of their meaningful conversation, but Jesus persisted, and the woman was open. What gets in the way of your honest conversation with Jesus?

What obstacles do you place there, or what inner resistance hinders you?

- When are you tempted to seek external signs to believe that Jesus is calling you? How do you put him to the test? How has your meditation on this reading influenced your approach to following Jesus?

## Ask God

Take some time for quiet reflection. In your own words, ask God to show you, through this Gospel reading, a clear path to the calling he has revealed to you.

## Think about the Main Idea

Look for the phrase in the reading that most catches your attention, and repeat it to yourself several times. You might also write it in a journal so that you can revisit it and think about it again.

## Create an Action Plan

Reading the Bible and praying with it can move us to change.

- How can this reading help you understand your calling better?
- What concrete action can you take to bring your prayer and meditation into daily life?

## Discussion Questions

1. This story includes one of the best-known passages in the Bible, John 3:16, which declares, "For God loved the world so much that he gave his only Son, so that everyone who believes in him may not die but have eternal life." Why do you think this verse has been so meaningful to so many people who follow Jesus?
2. Jews and Samaritans felt great animosity toward one another, and women were not respected in either culture. So Jesus crossed major boundaries by sharing his message of hope with a Samaritan woman. What cultural and ethnic barriers do you see today, and how might Jesus try to cross them? How might you cross them?

3. As Jesus continues to interact with the Samaritan woman, he is able to see parts of her life, of which she has been ashamed and has tried to keep from others. How do you think Jesus would respond to the parts of your life that you try to hide from others?

# 5

# Opposition Begins

Then Jesus went to Nazareth, where he had been brought up, and on the Sabbath he went as usual to the synagogue. He stood up to read the Scriptures and was handed the book of the prophet Isaiah. He unrolled the scroll and found the place where it is written, "The Spirit of the Lord is upon me, because he has chosen me to bring good news to the poor. He has sent me to proclaim liberty to the captives and recovery of sight to the blind, to set free the oppressed and announce that the time has come when the Lord will save his people."

Jesus rolled up the scroll, gave it back to the attendant, and sat down. All the people in the synagogue had their eyes fixed on him, as he said to them, "This passage of scripture has come true today, as you heard it being read."

They were all well impressed with him and marveled at the eloquent words that he spoke. They said, "Isn't he the son of Joseph?"

He said to them, "I am sure that you will quote this proverb to me, 'Doctor, heal yourself.' You will also tell me to do here in my hometown the same things you heard were done in Capernaum. I tell you this," Jesus added, "prophets are never welcomed in their hometown. Listen to me: it is true that there were many widows in Israel during the time of Elijah, when there was no rain for three and a half years and a severe famine spread throughout the whole land. Yet Elijah was not sent to anyone in Israel, but only to a widow living in Zarephath in the territory of Sidon. And there were many people suffering from a dreaded skin disease who lived in Israel during the time of the prophet Elisha; yet not one of them was healed, but only Naaman the Syrian."

When the people in the synagogue heard this, they were filled with anger. They rose up, dragged Jesus out of town, and took him to the top of the hill on which their town was built. They meant to throw him over the cliff, but he walked through the middle of the crowd and went his way. (Luke 4:16–30)

One day Jesus was standing on the shore of Lake Gennesaret while the people pushed their way up to him to listen to the word of God. He saw two boats pulled up on the beach; the fishermen had left them and were washing the nets. Jesus got into one of the boats—it belonged to Simon—and asked him to push off a little from the shore. Jesus sat in the boat and taught the crowd.

When he finished speaking, he said to Simon, "Push the boat out further to the deep water, and you and your partners let down your nets for a catch."

"Master," Simon answered, "we worked hard all night long and caught nothing. But if you say so, I will let down the nets." They let them down and caught such a large number of fish that the nets were about to break. So they motioned to their partners in the other boat to come and help them. They came and filled both boats so full of fish that the boats were about to sink. When Simon Peter saw what had happened, he fell on his knees before Jesus and said, "Go away from me, Lord! I am a sinful man!"

He and the others with him were all amazed at the large number of fish they had caught. The same was true of Simon's partners, James and John, the sons of Zebedee. Jesus said to Simon, "Don't be afraid; from now on you will be catching people."

They pulled the boats up on the beach, left everything, and followed Jesus. (Luke 5:1–11)

Jesus and his disciples came to the town of Capernaum, and on the next Sabbath Jesus went to the synagogue and began to teach. The people who heard him were amazed at the way he taught, for he wasn't like the teachers of the Law; instead, he taught with authority.

Just then a man with an evil spirit came into the synagogue and screamed, "What do you want with us, Jesus of Nazareth? Are you here to destroy us? I know who you are—you are God's holy messenger!"

Jesus ordered the spirit, "Be quiet, and come out of the man!"

The evil spirit shook the man hard, gave a loud scream, and came out of him. The people were all so amazed that they started saying to one another, "What is this? Is it some kind of new teaching? This man has authority to give orders to the evil spirits, and they obey him!"

And so the news about Jesus spread quickly everywhere in the province of Galilee.

Jesus and his disciples, including James and John, left the synagogue and went straight to the home of Simon and Andrew. Simon's mother-in-law was sick in bed with a fever, and as soon as Jesus arrived, he was told about her. He went to her, took her by the hand, and helped her up. The fever left her, and she began to wait on them.

After the sun had set and evening had come, people brought to Jesus all the sick and those who had demons. All the people of the town gathered in front of the house. Jesus healed many who were sick with all kinds of diseases and drove out many demons. He would not let the demons say anything, because they knew who he was.

Very early the next morning, long before daylight, Jesus got up and left the house. He went out of town to a lonely place, where he prayed. But Simon and his companions went out searching for him, and when they found him, they said, "Everyone is looking for you."

But Jesus answered, "We must go on to the other villages around here. I have to preach in them also, because that is why I came." (Mark 1:21–38)

Jesus went all over Galilee, teaching in the synagogues, preaching the Good News about the Kingdom, and healing people who had all kinds of disease and sickness. The news about him spread through the whole country of Syria, so that people brought to him all those who were sick, suffering from all kinds of diseases and disorders: people with demons, and epileptics, and paralytics—and Jesus healed them all. Large crowds followed him from Galilee and the Ten Towns, from Jerusalem, Judea, and the land on the other side of the Jordan. (Matthew 4:23–25)

Once Jesus was in a town where there was a man who was suffering from a dreaded skin disease. When he saw Jesus, he threw himself down and begged him, "Sir, if you want to, you can make me clean!"

Jesus reached out and touched him. "I do want to," he answered. "Be clean!" At once the disease left the man. Jesus ordered him, "Don't tell anyone, but go straight to the priest and let him examine you; then to prove to everyone that you are cured, offer the sacrifice as Moses ordered."

But the news about Jesus spread all the more widely, and crowds of people came to hear him and be healed from their diseases. But he would go away to lonely places, where he prayed.

One day when Jesus was teaching, some Pharisees and teachers of the Law were sitting there who had come from every town in Galilee and Judea and from Jerusalem. The power of the Lord was present for Jesus to heal the sick. Some men came carrying a paralyzed man on a bed, and they tried to carry him into the house and put him in front of Jesus. Because of the crowd, however, they could find no way to take him in. So they carried him up on the roof, made an opening in the tiles, and let him down on his bed into the middle of the group in front of Jesus. When Jesus saw how much faith they had, he said to the man, "Your sins are forgiven, my friend."

The teachers of the Law and the Pharisees began to say to themselves, "Who is this man who speaks such blasphemy! God is the only one who can forgive sins!"

Jesus knew their thoughts and said to them, "Why do you think such things? Is it easier to say, 'Your sins are forgiven you,' or to say, 'Get up and walk'? I will prove to you, then, that the Son of Man has authority on earth to forgive sins." So he said to the paralyzed man, "I tell you, get up, pick up your bed, and go home!"

At once the man got up in front of them all, took the bed he had been lying on, and went home, praising God. They were all completely amazed! Full of fear, they praised God, saying, "What marvelous things we have seen today!" (Luke 5:12–26)

Jesus left that place, and as he walked along, he saw a tax collector, named Matthew, sitting in his office. He said to him, "Follow me."

Matthew got up and followed him.

While Jesus was having a meal in Matthew's house, many tax collectors and other outcasts came and joined Jesus and his disciples at the table. Some Pharisees saw this and asked his disciples, "Why does your teacher eat with such people?"

Jesus heard them and answered, "People who are well do not need a doctor, but only those who are sick. Go and find out what is meant by the scripture that says: 'It is kindness that I want, not animal sacrifices.' I have not come to call respectable people, but outcasts." (Matthew 9:9–13)

Some people said to Jesus, "The disciples of John fast frequently and offer prayers, and the disciples of the Pharisees do the same; but your disciples eat and drink."

Jesus answered, "Do you think you can make the guests at a wedding party go without food as long as the bridegroom is with them? Of course not! But the day will come when the bridegroom will be taken away from them, and then they will fast."

Jesus also told them this parable: "You don't tear a piece off a new coat to patch up an old coat. If you do, you will have torn the new coat, and the piece of new cloth will not match the old. Nor do you pour new wine into used wineskins, because the new wine will burst the skins, the wine will pour out, and the skins will be ruined. Instead, new wine must be poured into fresh wineskins! And you don't want new wine after drinking old wine. 'The old is better,' you say." (Luke 5:33–39)

After this, Jesus went to Jerusalem for a religious festival. Near the Sheep Gate in Jerusalem there is a pool with five porches; in Hebrew it is called Bethzatha. A large crowd of sick people were lying on the porches—the blind, the lame, and the paralyzed. A man was there who had been sick for thirty-eight years. Jesus saw him lying there, and he knew that the man had been sick for such a long time; so he asked him, "Do you want to get well?"

The sick man answered, "Sir, I don't have anyone here to put me in the pool when the water is stirred up; while I am trying to get in, somebody else gets there first."

Jesus said to him, "Get up, pick up your mat, and walk." Immediately the man got well; he picked up his mat and started walking.

The day this happened was a Sabbath, so the Jewish authorities told the man who had been healed, "This is a Sabbath, and it is against our Law for you to carry your mat."

He answered, "The man who made me well told me to pick up my mat and walk."

They asked him, "Who is the man who told you to do this?"

But the man who had been healed did not know who Jesus was, for there was a crowd in that place, and Jesus had slipped away.

Afterward, Jesus found him in the Temple and said, "Listen, you are well now; so stop sinning or something worse may happen to you."

Then the man left and told the Jewish authorities that it was Jesus who had healed him.

So they began to persecute Jesus, because he had done this healing on a Sabbath. Jesus answered them, "My Father is always working, and I too must work."

This saying made the Jewish authorities all the more determined to kill him; not only had he broken the Sabbath law, but he had said that God was his own Father and in this way had made himself equal with God.

So Jesus answered them, "I tell you the truth: the Son can do nothing on his own; he does only what he sees his Father doing. What the Father does, the Son also does. For the Father loves the Son and shows him all that he himself is doing. He will show him even greater things to do than this, and you will all be amazed. Just as the Father raises the dead and gives them life, in the same way the Son gives life to those he wants to. Nor does the Father himself judge anyone. He has given his Son the full right to judge, so that all will honor the Son in the same way as they honor the Father. Whoever does not honor the Son does not honor the Father who sent him.

"I am telling you the truth: those who hear my words and believe in him who sent me have eternal life. They will not be judged, but have already passed from death to life. I am telling you the truth: the time is coming—the time has already come—when the dead will hear the voice of the Son of God, and those who hear it will come to life. Just as the Father is himself the source of life, in the same way he has made his Son to be the source of life. And he has given the Son the right to judge, because he is the Son of Man. Do not be surprised at this; the time is coming when all the dead will hear his voice and come out of their graves: those who have done good will rise and live, and those who have done evil will rise and be condemned.

"I can do nothing on my own authority; I judge only as God tells me, so my judgment is right, because I am not trying to do what I want, but only what he who sent me wants.

"If I testify on my own behalf, what I say is not to be accepted as real proof. But there is someone else who testifies on my behalf, and I know that what he says about me is true. John is the one to whom you sent your messengers, and he spoke on behalf of the truth. It is not that I must have a human witness; I say this only in order that you may be saved. John was like a lamp, burning and shining, and you were willing for a while to enjoy his light. But I have a witness on my behalf which is even greater than the witness that John gave: what I do, that is, the deeds my Father gave me to do, these speak on my behalf and show that the Father has sent me. And the Father, who sent me, also testifies on my behalf. You have never heard his voice or seen his face, and you do not keep his message in your hearts, for you do not believe in the one whom he sent. You study the Scriptures, because you think that in them you will find eternal life. And these very Scriptures speak about me! Yet you are not willing to come to me in order to have life.

"I am not looking for human praise. But I know what kind of people you are, and I know that you have no love for God in your hearts. I have come with my Father's authority, but you have not received me; when, however, someone comes with his own authority, you will receive him. You like to receive praise from one another, but you do not try to win praise from the one who alone is God; how, then, can you believe me? Do not think, however, that I am the one who will accuse you to my Father. Moses, in whom you have put your hope, is the very one who will accuse you. If you had really believed Moses, you would have believed me, because he wrote about me. But since you do not believe what he wrote, how can you believe what I say?" (John 5:1–47)

Jesus was walking through some wheat fields on a Sabbath. His disciples began to pick the heads of wheat, rub them in their hands, and eat the grain. Some Pharisees asked, "Why are you doing what our Law says you cannot do on the Sabbath?"

Jesus answered them, "Haven't you read what David did when he and his men were hungry? He went into the house of God, took the bread offered to God, ate it, and gave it also to his men. Yet it is against our Law for anyone except the priests to eat that bread."

And Jesus concluded, "The Son of Man is Lord of the Sabbath."

On another Sabbath, Jesus went into a synagogue and taught. A man was there whose right hand was paralyzed. Some teachers of the Law and some Pharisees wanted a reason to accuse Jesus of doing wrong, so they watched him closely to see if he would heal on the Sabbath. But Jesus knew their thoughts and said to the man, "Stand up and come here to the front." The man got up and stood there. Then Jesus said to them, "I ask you: What does our Law allow us to do on the Sabbath? To help or to harm? To save someone's life or destroy it?" He looked around at them all; then he said to the man, "Stretch out your hand." He did so, and his hand became well again.

They were filled with rage and began to discuss among themselves what they could do to Jesus. (Luke 6:1–11)

# Reflections and Questions

## About the Reading

This chapter begins with the interpretation of Holy Scripture. The passage that Jesus reads is from Isaiah. He speaks about the prophecy and explains that it is being fulfilled. Although many admire Jesus, others do not want to accept him, and the divisions begin. There are those who will accept his message, and those who will reject it.

Peter's encounter with Jesus is life changing. Seeing this miraculous catch, and recognizing himself as a sinner, Peter asks Jesus to leave him alone. Peter is afraid of contaminating the Master, but instead, Jesus cleanses Simon Peter and entrusts him with a mission.

Jesus' authority goes beyond that of the old laws, and that is why he is the Lord of the Sabbath, the holy day of rest. The discussions address why he heals people on the Sabbath, when it is not permitted. With this authority, he goes looking for the people who are most frowned upon, the public sinner, the tax collector who serves the foreign oppressors. One commentator on this calling explains, "He looked at them with mercy and chose them."

## Let's Meditate

God has a mission for each of us.

- Jesus comes to bring the Good News. Do you welcome him, or would you rather cling to your belief system, which, despite being Christian, is bound by rules and interpretations? Where do you feel you stand before Jesus, who is calling you to a conversion?

- Simon Peter asked Jesus to go away because he was afraid he would taint him with his sins. Do you also feel that your life and your sins hurt Jesus and the Church, and that is why you turn away from him? Do you realize that Jesus calls to you, despite your shortcomings?

- Can you, like the leper, reach out to Jesus with humility and say, "If you want to, you can make me clean"?

- In your own situation, how do you get up from your "stretcher," where you have been lying until now, and follow Christ?
- Poor Matthew is deeply ashamed of being a tax collector. He is unworthy in the eyes of the people, yet Jesus calls to him. Can you accept that, in spite of your public anguish, Jesus looks upon you with mercy and chooses you?

## Ask God

Take some time for quiet reflection. In your own words, ask God to show you, through this Gospel reading, a clear path to the calling he has revealed to you.

## Think about the Main Idea

Look for the phrase in the reading that most catches your attention, and repeat it to yourself several times. You might also write it in a journal so that you can revisit it and think about it again.

## Create an Action Plan

Reading the Bible and praying with it can move us to change.

- How can this reading help you understand your calling better?
- What concrete action can you take to bring your prayer and meditation into daily life?

## Discussion Questions

1. Imagine being in the synagogue and seeing Jesus read Isaiah 61:1, proclaiming that God has chosen him to "bring good news to the poor . . . and proclaim liberty to the captives." How do you think you would have felt? How would you have described what happened to friends who weren't there?
2. When a group of friends tore up a roof and lowered their disabled friend down in front of Jesus, he said two surprising things: "your sins are forgiven" and "get up, pick up your bed, and go home!" One seemed to be about spiritual healing and the other about physical

healing. Why do you think Jesus made both of those statements? What could it tell us about Jesus?

3. The friends of the man who was disabled lowered him through the roof to meet Jesus, who praised them for having great faith. Who do you know who has great faith? What (if anything) do you find appealing about their life and choices?

# 6

# Teaching the People

Jesus and his disciples went away to Lake Galilee, and a large crowd followed him. They had come from Galilee, from Judea, from Jerusalem, from the territory of Idumea, from the territory on the east side of the Jordan, and from the region around the cities of Tyre and Sidon. All these people came to Jesus because they had heard of the things he was doing. The crowd was so large that Jesus told his disciples to get a boat ready for him, so that the people would not crush him. He had healed many people, and all the sick kept pushing their way to him in order to touch him. And whenever the people who had evil spirits in them saw him, they would fall down before him and scream, "You are the Son of God!"

Jesus sternly ordered the evil spirits not to tell anyone who he was. (Mark 3:7–12) He did this so as to make come true what God had said through the prophet Isaiah: "Here is my servant, whom I have chosen, the one I love, and with whom I am pleased. I will send my Spirit upon him, and he will announce my judgment to the nations. He will not argue or shout, or make loud speeches in the streets. He will not break off a bent reed, nor put out a flickering lamp. He will persist until he causes justice to triumph, and on him all peoples will put their hope." (Matthew 12:17–21)

At that time Jesus went up a hill to pray and spent the whole night there praying to God. When day came, he called his disciples to him and chose twelve of them, whom he named apostles: Simon (whom he named Peter) and his brother Andrew; James and John, Philip and Bartholomew, Matthew and Thomas, James son of Alphaeus, and Simon (who was called the Patriot), Judas son of James, and Judas Iscariot, who became the traitor. (Luke 6:12–16)

Jesus saw the crowds and went up a hill, where he sat down. His disciples gathered around him, and he began to teach them:

"Happy are those who know they are spiritually poor; the Kingdom of heaven belongs to them!

"Happy are those who mourn; God will comfort them!

"Happy are those who are humble; they will receive what God has promised!

"Happy are those whose greatest desire is to do what God requires; God will satisfy them fully!

"Happy are those who are merciful to others; God will be merciful to them!

"Happy are the pure in heart; they will see God!

"Happy are those who work for peace; God will call them his children!

"Happy are those who are persecuted because they do what God requires; the Kingdom of heaven belongs to them! (Matthew 5:1–10)

"Happy are you when people hate you, reject you, insult you, and say that you are evil, all because of the Son of Man!

"Be glad when that happens and dance for joy, because a great reward is kept for you in heaven. For their ancestors did the very same things to the prophets.

"But how terrible for you who are rich now; you have had your easy life!

"How terrible for you who are full now; you will go hungry!

"How terrible for you who laugh now; you will mourn and weep!

"How terrible when all people speak well of you; their ancestors said the very same things about the false prophets. (Luke 6:22–26)

"You are like salt for the whole human race. But if salt loses its saltiness, there is no way to make it salty again. It has become worthless, so it is thrown out and people trample on it.

"You are like light for the whole world. A city built on a hill cannot be hid. No one lights a lamp and puts it under a bowl; instead it is put on the lampstand, where it gives light for everyone in the house. In the same way your light must shine before people, so that they will see the good things you do and praise your Father in heaven.

"Do not think that I have come to do away with the Law of Moses and the teachings of the prophets. I have not come to do away with them, but to make their teachings come true. Remember that as long as heaven and earth last, not the least point nor the smallest detail of the Law will be done away with—not until the end of all things. So then, whoever disobeys even the least important of the commandments and teaches others to do the same, will be least in the Kingdom of heaven. On the other hand, whoever obeys the Law and teaches others to do the same, will be great in the Kingdom of heaven. I tell you, then, that you will be able to enter the Kingdom of heaven only if you are more faithful than the teachers of the Law and the Pharisees in doing what God requires.

"You have heard that people were told in the past, 'Do not commit murder; anyone who does will be brought to trial.' But now I tell you: if you are angry with your brother you will be brought to trial, if you call your brother 'You good-for-nothing!' you will be brought before the Council, and if you call your brother a worthless fool you will be in danger of going to the fire of hell. So if you are about to offer your gift to God at the altar and there you remember that your brother has something against you, leave your gift there in front of the altar, go at once and make peace with your brother, and then come back and offer your gift to God.

"If someone brings a lawsuit against you and takes you to court, settle the dispute while there is time, before you get to court. Once you are there, you will be turned over to the judge, who will hand you over to the police, and you will be put in jail. There you will stay, I tell you, until you pay the last penny of your fine.

"You have heard that it was said, 'Do not commit adultery.' But now I tell you: anyone who looks at a woman and wants to possess her is guilty of committing adultery with her in his heart.

"So if your right eye causes you to sin, take it out and throw it away! It is much better for you to lose a part of your body than to have your whole body thrown into hell. If your right hand causes you to sin, cut it off and throw it away! It is much better for you to lose one of your limbs than to have your whole body go off to hell.

"It was also said, 'Anyone who divorces his wife must give her a written notice of divorce.' But now I tell you: if a man divorces his wife for any cause other than her unfaithfulness, then he is guilty of making her commit adultery if she marries again; and the man who marries her commits adultery also.

"You have also heard that people were told in the past, 'Do not break your promise, but do what you have vowed to the Lord to do.' But now I tell you: do not use any vow when you make a promise. Do not swear by heaven, for it is God's throne; nor by earth, for it is the resting place for his feet; nor by Jerusalem, for it is the city of the great King. Do not even swear by your head, because you cannot make a single hair white or black. Just say 'Yes' or 'No'—anything else you say comes from the Evil One.

"You have heard that it was said, 'An eye for an eye, and a tooth for a tooth.' But now I tell you: do not take revenge on someone who wrongs you. If anyone slaps you on the right cheek, let him slap your left cheek too. And if someone takes you to court to sue you for your shirt, let him have your coat as well. And if one of the occupation troops forces you to carry his pack one mile, carry it two miles. When someone asks you for something, give it to him; when someone wants to borrow something, lend it to him.

"You have heard that it was said, 'Love your friends, hate your enemies.' But now I tell you: love your enemies and pray for those who persecute you, so that you may become the children of your Father in heaven. For he makes his sun to shine on bad and good people alike, and gives rain to those who do good and to those who do evil. (Matthew 5:13–45)

"If you love only the people who love you, why should you receive a blessing? Even sinners love those who love them! And if you do good only to those who do good to you, why should you receive a blessing? Even sinners do that! And if you lend only to those from whom you hope to get it back, why should you receive a blessing? Even sinners lend to sinners, to get back the same amount! No! Love your enemies and do good to them; lend and expect nothing back. You will then have a great reward, and you will be children of the Most High God. For he is good to the ungrateful and the wicked. Be merciful just as your Father is merciful. (Luke 6:32–36)

"Make certain you do not perform your religious duties in public so that people will see what you do. If you do these things publicly, you will not have any reward from your Father in heaven.

"So when you give something to a needy person, do not make a big show of it, as the hypocrites do in the houses of worship and on the streets. They do it so that people will praise them. I assure you, they have already been paid in full. But when you help a needy person, do it in such a way that even your closest friend will not know about it. Then it will be a private matter. And your Father, who sees what you do in private, will reward you.

"When you pray, do not be like the hypocrites! They love to stand up and pray in the houses of worship and on the street corners, so that everyone will see them. I assure you, they have already been paid in full. But when you pray, go to your room, close the door, and pray to your Father, who is unseen. And your Father, who sees what you do in private, will reward you.

"When you pray, do not use a lot of meaningless words, as the pagans do, who think that their gods will hear them because their prayers are long. Do not be like them. Your Father already knows what you need before you ask him. This, then, is how you should pray:

"'Our Father in heaven: May your holy name be honored; may your Kingdom come; may your will be done on earth as it is in heaven. Give us today the food we need. Forgive us the wrongs we have done, as we forgive the wrongs that others have done to us. Do not bring us to hard testing, but keep us safe from the Evil One.'

"If you forgive others the wrongs they have done to you, your Father in heaven will also forgive you. But if you do not forgive others, then your Father will not forgive the wrongs you have done.

"And when you fast, do not put on a sad face as the hypocrites do. They neglect their appearance so that everyone will see that they are fasting. I assure you, they have already been paid in full. When you go without food, wash your face and comb your hair, so that others cannot know that you are fasting—only your Father, who is unseen, will know. And your Father, who sees what you do in private, will reward you.

"Do not store up riches for yourselves here on earth, where moths and rust destroy, and robbers break in and steal. Instead, store up riches for yourselves in heaven, where moths and rust cannot destroy, and robbers cannot break in and steal. For your heart will always be where your riches are.

"The eyes are like a lamp for the body. If your eyes are sound, your whole body will be full of light; but if your eyes are no good, your body will be in darkness. So if the light in you is darkness, how terribly dark it will be!

"You cannot be a slave of two masters; you will hate one and love the other; you will be loyal to one and despise the other. You cannot serve both God and money.

"This is why I tell you: do not be worried about the food and drink you need in order to stay alive, or about clothes for your body. After all, isn't life worth more than food? And isn't the body worth more than clothes? Look at the birds: they do not plant seeds, gather a harvest and put it in barns; yet your Father in heaven takes care of them! Aren't you worth much more than birds? Can any of you live a bit longer by worrying about it?

"And why worry about clothes? Look how the wild flowers grow: they do not work or make clothes for themselves. But I tell you that not even King Solomon with all his wealth had clothes as beautiful as one of these flowers. It is God who clothes the wild grass—grass that is here today and gone tomorrow, burned up in the oven. Won't he be all the more sure to clothe you? What little faith you have!

"So do not start worrying: 'Where will my food come from? or my drink? or my clothes?' These are the things the pagans are always concerned about. Your Father in heaven knows that you need all these things. Instead, be concerned above everything else with the Kingdom of God and with what he requires of you, and he will provide you with all these other things. So do not worry about tomorrow; it will have enough worries of its own. There is no need to add to the troubles each day brings. (Matthew 6:1–34)

"Do not judge others, so that God will not judge you, for God will judge you in the same way you judge others, and he will apply to you the same rules you apply to others. Why, then, do you look at the speck in your brother's eye and pay no attention to the log in your own eye? How dare you say to your brother, 'Please, let me take that speck out of your eye,' when you have a log in your own eye? You hypocrite! First take the log out of your own eye, and then you will be able to see clearly to take the speck out of your brother's eye.

"Do not give what is holy to dogs—they will only turn and attack you. Do not throw your pearls in front of pigs—they will only trample them underfoot.

"Ask, and you will receive; seek, and you will find; knock, and the door will be opened to you. For everyone who asks will receive, and anyone who seeks will find, and the door will be opened to those who knock. Would any of you who are fathers give your son a stone when he asks for bread? Or would you give him a snake when he asks for a fish? As bad as you are, you know how to give good things to your children. How much more, then, will your Father in heaven give good things to those who ask him!

"Do for others what you want them to do for you: this is the meaning of the Law of Moses and of the teachings of the prophets.

"Go in through the narrow gate, because the gate to hell is wide and the road that leads to it is easy, and there are many who travel it. But the gate to life is narrow and the way that leads to it is hard, and there are few people who find it.

"Be on your guard against false prophets; they come to you looking like sheep on the outside, but on the inside they are really like wild wolves. You will know them by what they do. Thorn bushes do not bear grapes, and briers do not bear figs. A healthy tree bears good fruit, but a poor tree bears bad fruit. A healthy tree cannot bear bad fruit, and a poor tree cannot bear good fruit. And any tree that does not bear good fruit is cut down and thrown in the fire. So then, you will know the false prophets by what they do. (Matthew 7:1–20)

"A good person brings good out of the treasure of good things in his heart; a bad person brings bad out of his treasure of bad things. For the mouth speaks what the heart is full of.

"Why do you call me, 'Lord, Lord,' and yet don't do what I tell you? (Luke 6:45–46) Not everyone who calls me 'Lord, Lord' will enter the Kingdom of heaven, but only those who do what my Father in heaven wants them to do. When the Judgment Day comes, many will say to me, 'Lord, Lord! In your name we spoke God's message, by your name we drove out many demons and performed many miracles!' Then I will say to them, 'I never knew you. Get away from me, you wicked people!'

"So then, anyone who hears these words of mine and obeys them is like a wise man who built his house on rock. The rain poured down, the rivers flooded over, and the wind blew hard against that house. But it did not fall, because it was built on rock.

"But anyone who hears these words of mine and does not obey them is like a foolish man who built his house on sand. The rain poured down, the rivers flooded over, the wind blew hard against that house, and it fell. And what a terrible fall that was!"

When Jesus finished saying these things, the crowd was amazed at the way he taught. He wasn't like the teachers of the Law; instead, he taught with authority. (Matthew 7:21–29)

# Reflections and Questions

### About the Reading

It is interesting to note at the beginning of this reading how the evil spirits acknowledge Jesus by telling him, "You are the Son of God!" And he is. He has full authority to choose the twelve followers whom he calls apostles. It is Jesus who takes it upon himself to choose them.

It is with this authority he gives a great sermon on guidelines for our true happiness. He concludes that his disciples must be the "salt" to prevent the world from rotting, and they must be the "light" to illuminate it. That will be our testimony for the world to believe: a new way of life that brings the ultimate fulfillment of the law. The topics that follow in Jesus' sermon are vital, such as our love for everyone—even our enemies—our prayers expressed as a dialogue with the Father, and the relationship Jesus' disciples should have with the things of this world.

His teaching produces a vital change that will be seen in the fruit of our lives. If we call Jesus "Lord," then we must do what he says. Listening to and obeying Jesus is like building our house on a rock foundation.

### Let's Meditate

God has a mission for each of us.

- Do you believe that Jesus personally calls to you for a mission that no one else but you can carry out in his name? What are you doing to know this mission and carry it out?

- When you read the new ways in which Jesus defines happiness, how do you compare those ways to the world's way of thinking? How do you pay attention to each one of these ways to happiness, or blessedness? Which do you think are harder for you, and how can you better conform your life to Jesus' way?

- On the subject of forgiveness and love, to what extent is it something that transforms you from within? How can you move from knowing about forgiveness to forgiving others—or asking them to forgive you?

- How is your prayer life? Is it a practice that you adopt daily? How can you improve it?

- How do you go from hearing what Jesus says to doing it? What are things you do to show that change?

## Ask God

Take some time for quiet reflection. In your own words, ask God to show you, through this Gospel reading, a clear path to the calling he has revealed to you.

## Think about the Main Idea

Look for the phrase in the reading that most catches your attention, and repeat it to yourself several times. You might also write it in a journal so that you can revisit it and think about it again.

## Create an Action Plan

Reading the Bible and praying with it can move us to change.

- How can this reading help you understand your calling better?
- What concrete action can you take to bring your prayer and meditation into daily life?

## Discussion Questions

1. When Jesus teaches a crowd on a hill, he makes a number of promises that those who are needy, sad, humble, merciful, and pure and who suffer for doing what is right will be "happy." If you had been among the crowd and heard all of Jesus' amazing (but counterintuitive) promises about being "happy" in these circumstances, which would stand out the most to you, and why?
2. Perhaps Jesus' most radical teaching is that we are to "love" our enemies and "pray for" those who hurt us. Why would Jesus want us to do this? As you think about your own enemies or those who have hurt you, how could you take a first step toward following Jesus' teaching?
3. In the midst of our worries of all sizes, Jesus tells us *not* to worry, because God will take care of our needs, and that it's more important to focus on putting God's kingdom first. What is causing you anxiety right now, and how can you ask God to help you with that?

# 7

# Accused of Using Evil

When Jesus had finished saying all these things to the people, he went to Capernaum. A Roman officer there had a servant who was very dear to him; the man was sick and about to die. When the officer heard about Jesus, he sent some Jewish elders to ask him to come and heal his servant. They came to Jesus and begged him earnestly, "This man really deserves your help. He loves our people and he himself built a synagogue for us."

So Jesus went with them. He was not far from the house when the officer sent friends to tell him, "Sir, don't trouble yourself. I do not deserve to have you come into my house, neither do I consider myself worthy to come to you in person. Just give the order, and my servant will get well. I, too, am a man placed under the authority of superior officers, and I have soldiers under me. I order this one, 'Go!' and he goes; I order that one, 'Come!' and he comes; and I order my slave, 'Do this!' and he does it."

Jesus was surprised when he heard this; he turned around and said to the crowd following him, "I tell you, I have never found faith like this, not even in Israel!"

The messengers went back to the officer's house and found his servant well.

Soon afterward Jesus went to a town named Nain, accompanied by his disciples and a large crowd. Just as he arrived at the gate of the town, a funeral procession was coming out. The dead man was the only son of a woman who was a widow, and a large crowd from the town was with her. When the Lord saw her, his heart was filled with pity for her, and he said to her, "Don't cry." Then he walked over and touched the coffin, and the men carrying it stopped. Jesus said, "Young man! Get up, I tell you!" The dead man sat up and began to talk, and Jesus gave him back to his mother.

They all were filled with fear and praised God. "A great prophet has appeared among us!" they said; "God has come to save his people!"

This news about Jesus went out through all the country and the surrounding territory.

When John's disciples told him about all these things, he called two of them and sent them to the Lord to ask him, "Are you the one John said was going to come, or should we expect someone else?"

When they came to Jesus, they said, "John the Baptist sent us to ask if you are the one he said was going to come, or should we expect someone else?"

At that very time Jesus healed many people from their sicknesses, diseases, and evil spirits, and gave sight to many blind people. He answered John's messengers, "Go back and tell John what you have seen and heard: the blind can see, the lame can walk, those who suffer from dreaded skin diseases are made clean, the deaf can hear, the dead are raised to life, and the Good News is preached to the poor. How happy are those who have no doubts about me!"

After John's messengers had left, Jesus began to speak about him to the crowds: "When you went out to John in the desert, what did you expect to see? A blade of grass bending in the wind? What did you go out to see? A man dressed up in fancy clothes? People who dress like that and live in luxury are found in palaces! Tell me, what did you go out to see? A prophet? Yes indeed, but you saw much more than a prophet. For John is the one of whom the scripture says: 'God said, I will send my messenger ahead of you to open the way for you.' I tell you," Jesus added, "John is greater than anyone who has ever lived. But the one who is least in the Kingdom of God is greater than John."

All the people heard him; they and especially the tax collectors were the ones who had obeyed God's righteous demands and had been baptized by

John. But the Pharisees and the teachers of the Law rejected God's purpose for themselves and refused to be baptized by John.

Jesus continued, "Now to what can I compare the people of this day? What are they like? They are like children sitting in the marketplace. One group shouts to the other, 'We played wedding music for you, but you wouldn't dance! We sang funeral songs, but you wouldn't cry!' John the Baptist came, and he fasted and drank no wine, and you said, 'He has a demon in him!' The Son of Man came, and he ate and drank, and you said, 'Look at this man! He is a glutton and wine drinker, a friend of tax collectors and other outcasts!' God's wisdom, however, is shown to be true by all who accept it." (Luke 7:1–35)

At that time Jesus said, "Father, Lord of heaven and earth! I thank you because you have shown to the unlearned what you have hidden from the wise and learned. Yes, Father, this was how you were pleased to have it happen.

"My Father has given me all things. No one knows the Son except the Father, and no one knows the Father except the Son and those to whom the Son chooses to reveal him.

"Come to me, all of you who are tired from carrying heavy loads, and I will give you rest. Take my yoke and put it on you, and learn from me, because I am gentle and humble in spirit; and you will find rest. For the yoke I will give you is easy, and the load I will put on you is light." (Matthew 11:25–30)

Some time later Jesus traveled through towns and villages, preaching the Good News about the Kingdom of God. The twelve disciples went with him, and so did some women who had been healed of evil spirits and diseases: Mary (who was called Magdalene), from whom seven demons had been driven out; Joanna, whose husband Chuza was an officer in Herod's court; and Susanna, and many other women who used their own resources to help Jesus and his disciples. (Luke 8:1–3)

Then Jesus went home. Again such a large crowd gathered that Jesus and his disciples had no time to eat. When his family heard about it, they set out to take charge of him, because people were saying, "He's gone mad!" (Mark 3:20–21)

Then some people brought to Jesus a man who was blind and could not talk because he had a demon. Jesus healed the man, so that he was able to talk and see. The crowds were all amazed at what Jesus had done. "Could he be the Son of David?" they asked.

When the Pharisees heard this, they replied, "He drives out demons only because their ruler Beelzebul gives him power to do so."

Jesus knew what they were thinking, and so he said to them, "Any country that divides itself into groups which fight each other will not last very long. And any town or family that divides itself into groups which fight each other will fall apart. So if one group is fighting another in Satan's kingdom, this means that it is already divided into groups and will soon fall apart! You say that I drive out demons because Beelzebul gives me the power to do so. Well, then, who gives your followers the power to drive them out? What your own followers do proves that you are wrong! No, it is not Beelzebul, but God's Spirit, who gives me the power to drive out demons, which proves that the Kingdom of God has already come upon you.

"No one can break into a strong man's house and take away his belongings unless he first ties up the strong man; then he can plunder his house.

"Anyone who is not for me is really against me; anyone who does not help me gather is really scattering. For this reason I tell you: people can be forgiven any sin and any evil thing they say; but whoever says evil things against the Holy Spirit will not be forgiven. Anyone who says something against the Son of Man can be forgiven; but whoever says something against the Holy Spirit will not be forgiven—now or ever.

"To have good fruit you must have a healthy tree; if you have a poor tree, you will have bad fruit. A tree is known by the kind of fruit it bears. You snakes—how can you say good things when you are evil? For the mouth speaks what the heart is full of. A good person brings good things out of a treasure of good things; a bad person brings bad things out of a treasure of bad things.

"You can be sure that on the Judgment Day you will have to give account of every useless word you have ever spoken. Your words will be used to judge you—to declare you either innocent or guilty." (Matthew 12:22–37)

When Jesus had said this, a woman spoke up from the crowd and said to him, "How happy is the woman who bore you and nursed you!"

But Jesus answered, "Rather, how happy are those who hear the word of God and obey it!"

As the people crowded around Jesus, he went on to say, "How evil are the people of this day! They ask for a miracle, but none will be given them except the miracle of Jonah. In the same way that the prophet Jonah was a sign for the people of Nineveh, so the Son of Man will be a sign for the people of this day. (Luke 11:27–30) In the same way that Jonah spent three days and nights in the big fish, so will the Son of Man spend three days and nights in the depths of the earth. On the Judgment Day the people of Nineveh will stand up and accuse you, because they turned from their sins when they heard Jonah preach; and I tell you that there is something here greater than Jonah! On the Judgment Day the Queen of Sheba will stand up and accuse you, because she traveled all the way from her country to listen to King Solomon's wise teaching; and I assure you that there is something here greater than Solomon!

"When an evil spirit goes out of a person, it travels over dry country looking for a place to rest. If it can't find one, it says to itself, 'I will go back to my house.' So it goes back and finds the house empty, clean, and all fixed up. Then it goes out and brings along seven other spirits even worse than itself, and they come and live there. So when it is all over, that person is in worse shape than at the beginning. This is what will happen to the evil people of this day."

Jesus was still talking to the people when his mother and brothers arrived. They stood outside, asking to speak with him. So one of the people there said to him, "Look, your mother and brothers are standing outside, and they want to speak with you."

Jesus answered, "Who is my mother? Who are my brothers?" Then he pointed to his disciples and said, "Look! Here are my mother and my brothers! Whoever does what my Father in heaven wants is my brother, my sister, and my mother." (Matthew 12:40–50)

That same day Jesus left the house and went to the lakeside, where he sat down to teach. The crowd that gathered around him was so large that he got into a boat and sat in it, while the crowd stood on the shore. He used parables to tell them many things.

Jesus said, "Once there was a man who went out to sow grain. As he scattered the seed in the field, some of it fell along the path, and the birds came and ate it up. Some of it fell on rocky ground, where there was little soil. The seeds soon sprouted, because the soil wasn't deep. But when the sun came up, it burned the young plants; and because the roots had not grown deep enough, the plants soon dried up. Some of the seed fell among thorn bushes, which grew up and choked the plants. But some seeds fell in good soil, and the plants bore grain: some had one hundred grains, others sixty, and others thirty."

And Jesus concluded, "Listen, then, if you have ears!"

Then the disciples came to Jesus and asked him, "Why do you use parables when you talk to the people?"

Jesus answered, "The knowledge about the secrets of the Kingdom of heaven has been given to you, but not to them. For the person who has something will be given more, so that he will have more than enough; but the person who has nothing will have taken away from him even the little he has. The reason I use parables in talking to them is that they look, but do not see, and they listen, but do not hear or understand.

"So the prophecy of Isaiah applies to them: 'This people will listen and listen, but not understand; they will look and look, but not see, because their minds are dull, and they have stopped up their ears and have closed their eyes. Otherwise, their eyes would see, their ears would hear, their minds would understand, and they would turn to me, says God, and I would heal them.'

"As for you, how fortunate you are! Your eyes see and your ears hear. I assure you that many prophets and many of God's people wanted very much to see what you see, but they could not, and to hear what you hear, but they did not." (Matthew 13:1–17)

Then Jesus asked them, "Don't you understand this parable? How, then, will you ever understand any parable? The sower sows God's message. Some people are like the seeds that fall along the path; as soon as they hear the message, Satan comes and takes it away. Other people are like the seeds that fall on rocky ground. As soon as they hear the message, they receive it gladly. But it does not sink deep into them, and they don't last long. So when trouble or persecution comes because of the message, they give up at once. Other people are like the seeds sown among the thorn bushes. These are the ones who hear the message, but the worries about this life, the love for riches, and all other kinds of desires crowd in and choke the message, and they don't bear fruit. But other people are like seeds sown in good soil. They hear the message, accept it, and bear fruit: some thirty, some sixty, and some one hundred." (Mark 4:13–20)

Jesus told them another parable: "The Kingdom of heaven is like this. A man sowed good seed in his field. One night, when everyone was asleep, an enemy came and sowed weeds among the wheat and went away. When the plants grew and the heads of grain began to form, then the weeds showed up. The man's servants came to him and said, 'Sir, it was good seed you sowed in your field; where did the weeds come from?' 'It was some enemy who did this,' he answered. 'Do you want us to go and pull up the weeds?' they asked him. 'No,' he answered, 'because as you gather the weeds you might pull up some of the wheat along with them. Let the wheat and the weeds both grow together until harvest. Then I will tell the harvest workers to pull up the weeds first, tie them in bundles and burn them, and then to gather in the wheat and put it in my barn.'" (Matthew 13:24–30)

Jesus went on to say, "The Kingdom of God is like this. A man scatters seed in his field. He sleeps at night, is up and about during the day, and all the while the seeds are sprouting and growing. Yet he does not know how it happens. The soil itself makes the plants grow and bear fruit; first the tender stalk appears, then the head, and finally the head full of grain. When the grain is ripe, the man starts cutting it with his sickle, because harvest time has come.

"What shall we say the Kingdom of God is like?" asked Jesus. "What parable shall we use to explain it? It is like this. A man takes a mustard seed, the smallest seed in the world, and plants it in the ground. After a while it grows up and becomes the biggest of all plants. It puts out such large branches that the birds come and make their nests in its shade." (Mark 4:26–32)

When Jesus had left the crowd and gone indoors, his disciples came to him and said, "Tell us what the parable about the weeds in the field means."

Jesus answered, "The man who sowed the good seed is the Son of Man; the field is the world; the good seed is the people who belong to the Kingdom; the weeds are the people who belong to the Evil One; and the enemy who sowed the weeds is the Devil. The harvest is the end of the age, and the harvest workers are angels. Just as the weeds are gathered up and burned in the fire, so the same thing will happen at the end of the age: the Son of Man will send out his angels to gather up out of his Kingdom all those who cause people to sin and all others who do evil things, and they will throw them into the fiery furnace, where they will cry and gnash their teeth. Then God's people will shine like the sun in their Father's Kingdom. Listen, then, if you have ears!

"The Kingdom of heaven is like this. A man happens to find a treasure hidden in a field. He covers it up again, and is so happy that he goes and sells everything he has, and then goes back and buys that field.

"Also, the Kingdom of heaven is like this. A man is looking for fine pearls, and when he finds one that is unusually fine, he goes and sells everything he has, and buys that pearl.

"And the Kingdom of heaven is like this. Some fishermen throw their net out in the lake and catch all kinds of fish. When the net is full, they pull it to shore and sit down to divide the fish: the good ones go into the buckets, the worthless ones are thrown away. It will be like this at the end of the age: the angels will go out and gather up the evil people from among the good and will throw them into the fiery furnace, where they will cry and gnash their teeth.

"Do you understand these things?" Jesus asked them.

"Yes," they answered.

So he replied, "This means, then, that every teacher of the Law who becomes a disciple in the Kingdom of heaven is like a homeowner who takes new and old things out of his storage room." (Matthew 13:36–52)

Jesus preached his message to the people, using many other parables like these; he told them as much as they could understand. He would not speak to them without using parables, but when he was alone with his disciples, he would explain everything to them. (Mark 4:33–34)

# Reflections and Questions

## About the Reading

Notice that it was a Roman officer who acknowledged Jesus' authority. He said to Jesus, "Just give the order," because the word of Christ has power. Later on, Jesus continues his journey and comes across a funeral procession for a young man, the son of a widow. Life meets death, and the Life brings the young man back from death. It is a call to live again. It is such a momentous happening that John the Baptist sends messengers to ask if Jesus is the One who was prophesied to come. According to Jesus, John is "greater than anyone who has ever lived"; yet, the least person in God's Kingdom is greater than John.

Jesus announces in prayer, "I thank you because you have shown it to the unlearned." Jesus does not seek out the wise or powerful, nor the current religious leaders; he looks for simple people. Jesus delivers from evil with the power of good. An evil kingdom that divides itself will fall apart. The religious leaders' envy of Jesus' power is clear.

He asks, "Who is my mother, and who are my brothers?" and answers: it is everyone who listens to the word of God and puts it into practice. That is why he speaks in parables, to make his message understandable. He and his disciples sow the message, but evil people also sow their own seeds. The disciples ask for his help to understand.

## Let's Meditate

God has a mission for each of us.

- It's time to ask yourself directly, *Am I convinced that the Word of Jesus has power? How does it manifest in my life? Do I believe that, with his authority, Jesus calls me to follow him? What is that path for me?*

- It did not matter to Jesus that the young man was already dead; he called him to life. At what times have you felt almost dead in some way? Do you think Jesus has a word for you that can raise you from your situation of death, of sin, or of apathy?

- Jesus reveals himself to people who are humble. Do you want to understand Jesus? Come before him with humility and ask for that gift.
- "Whoever hears the Word of God and puts it into practice." Could Jesus be describing you with these words?
- How do you see yourself in the parable of the good seed and the weeds? Both are sown in your life; can you identify them?

### Ask God

Take some time for quiet reflection. In your own words, ask God to show you, through this Gospel reading, a clear path to the calling he has revealed to you.

### Think about the Main Idea

Look for the phrase in the reading that most catches your attention, and repeat it to yourself several times. You might also write it in a journal so that you can revisit it and think about it again.

### Create an Action Plan

Reading the Bible and praying with it can move us to change.

- How can this reading help you understand your calling better?
- What concrete action can you take to bring your prayer and meditation into daily life?

### Discussion Questions

1. Jesus praises the Roman officer's faith as one of the greatest he has ever seen. What is it about the Roman officer's description of authority that shows his great faith? In what ways would you like your faith to be like the Roman officer's?

2. When Jesus hears that his mother and brothers are standing outside, he says, "Whoever does what my Father in heaven wants is my brother, my sister, and my mother." Who do you consider your family, and what determines that? How does Jesus' definition of family challenge or expand your own definition of family?

3. Jesus tells a story of a farmer who sows seeds in four different places: along the road, in rocky soil, in thorny soil, and in good soil. If the seed is God's message, which of these four soils best describes you? Why do you think God is so generous to sow seeds in all kinds of soil?

# 8

# Calming a Storm

One day Jesus got into a boat with his disciples and said to them, "Let us go across to the other side of the lake." So they started out. As they were sailing, Jesus fell asleep. Suddenly a strong wind blew down on the lake, and the boat began to fill with water, so that they were all in great danger. The disciples went to Jesus and woke him up, saying, "Master, Master! We are about to die!"

Jesus got up and gave an order to the wind and to the stormy water; they quieted down, and there was a great calm. Then he said to the disciples, "Where is your faith?"

But they were amazed and afraid, and said to one another, "Who is this man? He gives orders to the winds and waves, and they obey him!" (Luke 8:22–25)

Jesus and his disciples arrived on the other side of Lake Galilee, in the territory of Gerasa. As soon as Jesus got out of the boat, he was met by a man who came out of the burial caves there. This man had an evil spirit in him and lived among the tombs. Nobody could keep him tied with chains any more; many times his feet and his hands had been tied, but every time he broke the chains and smashed the irons on his feet. He was too strong for anyone to control him. Day and night he wandered among the tombs and through the hills, screaming and cutting himself with stones.

He was some distance away when he saw Jesus; so he ran, fell on his knees before him, and screamed in a loud voice, "Jesus, Son of the Most High God!

What do you want with me? For God's sake, I beg you, don't punish me!" (He said this because Jesus was saying, "Evil spirit, come out of this man!")

So Jesus asked him, "What is your name?"

The man answered, "My name is 'Mob'—there are so many of us!" And he kept begging Jesus not to send the evil spirits out of that region.

There was a large herd of pigs near by, feeding on a hillside. So the spirits begged Jesus, "Send us to the pigs, and let us go into them." He let them go, and the evil spirits went out of the man and entered the pigs. The whole herd—about two thousand pigs in all—rushed down the side of the cliff into the lake and was drowned.

The men who had been taking care of the pigs ran away and spread the news in the town and among the farms. People went out to see what had happened, and when they came to Jesus, they saw the man who used to have the mob of demons in him. He was sitting there, clothed and in his right mind; and they were all afraid. Those who had seen it told the people what had happened to the man with the demons, and about the pigs.

So they asked Jesus to leave their territory.

As Jesus was getting into the boat, the man who had had the demons begged him, "Let me go with you!"

But Jesus would not let him. Instead, he told him, "Go back home to your family and tell them how much the Lord has done for you and how kind he has been to you."

So the man left and went all through the Ten Towns, telling what Jesus had done for him. And all who heard it were amazed.


Jesus went back across to the other side of the lake. There at the lakeside a large crowd gathered around him. Jairus, an official of the local synagogue, arrived, and when he saw Jesus, he threw himself down at his feet and begged him earnestly, "My little daughter is very sick. Please come and place your hands on her, so that she will get well and live!"

Then Jesus started off with him. So many people were going along with Jesus that they were crowding him from every side.

There was a woman who had suffered terribly from severe bleeding for twelve years, even though she had been treated by many doctors. She had spent all her money, but instead of getting better she got worse all the time. She had heard about Jesus, so she came in the crowd behind him, saying to herself, "If I just touch his clothes, I will get well."

She touched his cloak, and her bleeding stopped at once; and she had the feeling inside herself that she was healed of her trouble. At once Jesus knew that power had gone out of him, so he turned around in the crowd and asked, "Who touched my clothes?"

His disciples answered, "You see how the people are crowding you; why do you ask who touched you?"

But Jesus kept looking around to see who had done it. The woman realized what had happened to her, so she came, trembling with fear, knelt at his feet, and told him the whole truth. Jesus said to her, "My daughter, your faith has made you well. Go in peace, and be healed of your trouble."

While Jesus was saying this, some messengers came from Jairus' house and told him, "Your daughter has died. Why bother the Teacher any longer?"

Jesus paid no attention to what they said, but told him, "Don't be afraid, only believe." Then he did not let anyone else go on with him except Peter and James and his brother John. They arrived at Jairus' house, where Jesus saw the confusion and heard all the loud crying and wailing. He went in and said to them, "Why all this confusion? Why are you crying? The child is not dead—she is only sleeping!"

They started making fun of him, so he put them all out, took the child's father and mother and his three disciples, and went into the room where the child was lying. He took her by the hand and said to her, "*Talitha, koum,*" which means, "Little girl, I tell you to get up!"

She got up at once and started walking around. (She was twelve years old.) When this happened, they were completely amazed. But Jesus gave them strict orders not to tell anyone, and he said, "Give her something to eat." (Mark 5:1–43)

Jesus left that place, and as he walked along, two blind men started following him. "Have mercy on us, Son of David!" they shouted.

When Jesus had gone indoors, the two blind men came to him, and he asked them, "Do you believe that I can heal you?"

"Yes, sir!" they answered.

Then Jesus touched their eyes and said, "Let it happen, then, just as you believe!"—and their sight was restored. Jesus spoke sternly to them, "Don't tell this to anyone!"

But they left and spread the news about Jesus all over that part of the country.

As the men were leaving, some people brought to Jesus a man who could not talk because he had a demon. But as soon as the demon was driven out, the man started talking, and everyone was amazed. "We have never seen anything like this in Israel!" they exclaimed.

But the Pharisees said, "It is the chief of the demons who gives Jesus the power to drive out demons." (Matthew 9:27–34)

Jesus went back to his hometown, followed by his disciples. On the Sabbath he began to teach in the synagogue. Many people were there; and when they heard him, they were all amazed. "Where did he get all this?" they asked. "What wisdom is this that has been given him? How does he perform miracles? Isn't he the carpenter, the son of Mary, and the brother of James, Joseph, Judas, and Simon? Aren't his sisters living here?" And so they rejected him.

Jesus said to them, "Prophets are respected everywhere except in their own hometown and by their relatives and their family."

He was not able to perform any miracles there, except that he placed his hands on a few sick people and healed them. He was greatly surprised, because the people did not have faith. (Mark 6:1–6)

Jesus went around visiting all the towns and villages. He taught in the synagogues, preached the Good News about the Kingdom, and healed people with every kind of disease and sickness. As he saw the crowds, his heart was filled with pity for them, because they were worried and helpless, like sheep without a shepherd. So he said to his disciples, "The harvest is large, but there are few workers to gather it in. Pray to the owner of the harvest that he will send out workers to gather in his harvest." (Matthew 9:35–38)

Jesus called the twelve disciples together and gave them power and authority to drive out all demons and to cure diseases. Then he sent them out to preach the Kingdom of God and to heal the sick. (Luke 9:1–2) They were sent out with the following instructions:

"Do not go to any Gentile territory or any Samaritan towns. Instead, you are to go to the lost sheep of the people of Israel. Go and preach, 'The Kingdom of heaven is near!' Heal the sick, bring the dead back to life, heal those who suffer from dreaded skin diseases, and drive out demons. You have received without paying, so give without being paid. Do not carry any gold, silver, or copper money in your pockets; do not carry a beggar's bag for the trip or an extra shirt or shoes or a walking stick. Workers should be given what they need.

"When you come to a town or village, go in and look for someone who is willing to welcome you, and stay with him until you leave that place. When you go into a house, say, 'Peace be with you.' If the people in that house welcome you, let your greeting of peace remain; but if they do not welcome you, then take back your greeting. And if some home or town will not welcome you or listen to you, then leave that place and shake the dust off your feet. I assure you that on the Judgment Day God will show more mercy to the people of Sodom and Gomorrah than to the people of that town!

"Listen! I am sending you out just like sheep to a pack of wolves. You must be as cautious as snakes and as gentle as doves. Watch out, for there will be those who will arrest you and take you to court, and they will whip you in the synagogues. For my sake you will be brought to trial before rulers and kings, to tell the Good News to them and to the Gentiles. When they bring you to trial, do not worry about what you are going to say or how you will say it; when the time comes, you will be given what you will say. For the words you will speak will not be yours; they will come from the Spirit of your Father speaking through you.

"People will hand over their own brothers to be put to death, and fathers will do the same to their children; children will turn against their parents and have them put to death. Everyone will hate you because of me. But whoever holds out to the end will be saved. When they persecute you in one town, run away to another one. I assure you that you will not finish your work in all the towns of Israel before the Son of Man comes.

"No pupil is greater than his teacher; no slave is greater than his master. So a pupil should be satisfied to become like his teacher, and a slave like his master. If the head of the family is called Beelzebul, the members of the family will be called even worse names!

"So do not be afraid of people. Whatever is now covered up will be uncovered, and every secret will be made known. What I am telling you in the dark you must repeat in broad daylight, and what you have heard in private you must announce from the housetops. Do not be afraid of those who kill the body but cannot kill the soul; rather be afraid of God, who can destroy both body and soul in hell. For only a penny you can buy two sparrows, yet not one sparrow falls to the ground without your Father's consent. As for you, even the hairs of your head have all been counted. So do not be afraid; you are worth much more than many sparrows!

"Those who declare publicly that they belong to me, I will do the same for them before my Father in heaven. But those who reject me publicly, I will reject before my Father in heaven.

"Do not think that I have come to bring peace to the world. No, I did not come to bring peace, but a sword. I came to set sons against their fathers, daughters against their mothers, daughters-in-law against their mothers-in-law; your worst enemies will be the members of your own family.

"Those who love their father or mother more than me are not fit to be my disciples; those who love their son or daughter more than me are not fit to be my disciples. Those who do not take up their cross and follow in my steps are not fit to be my disciples. Those who try to gain their own life will lose it; but those who lose their life for my sake will gain it.

"Whoever welcomes you welcomes me; and whoever welcomes me welcomes the one who sent me. Whoever welcomes God's messenger because he is God's messenger, will share in his reward. And whoever welcomes a good man because he is good, will share in his reward. You can be sure that whoever gives even a drink of cold water to one of the least of these my followers because he is my follower, will certainly receive a reward." (Matthew 10:5–42)

Now King Herod heard about all this, because Jesus' reputation had spread everywhere. Some people were saying, "John the Baptist has come back to life! That is why he has this power to perform miracles."

Others, however, said, "He is Elijah."

Others said, "He is a prophet, like one of the prophets of long ago."

When Herod heard it, he said, "He is John the Baptist! I had his head cut off, but he has come back to life!" Herod himself had ordered John's arrest, and he had him tied up and put in prison. Herod did this because of Herodias, whom he had married, even though she was the wife of his brother Philip. John the Baptist kept telling Herod, "It isn't right for you to marry your brother's wife!"

So Herodias held a grudge against John and wanted to kill him, but she could not because of Herod. Herod was afraid of John because he knew that John was a good and holy man, and so he kept him safe. He liked to listen to him, even though he became greatly disturbed every time he heard him.

Finally Herodias got her chance. It was on Herod's birthday, when he gave a feast for all the top government officials, the military chiefs, and the leading citizens of Galilee. The daughter of Herodias came in and danced, and pleased Herod and his guests. So the king said to the girl, "What would you like to have? I will give you anything you want." With many vows he said to her, "I swear that I will give you anything you ask for, even as much as half my kingdom!"

So the girl went out and asked her mother, "What shall I ask for?"

"The head of John the Baptist," she answered.

The girl hurried back at once to the king and demanded, "I want you to give me here and now the head of John the Baptist on a plate!"

This made the king very sad, but he could not refuse her because of the vows he had made in front of all his guests. So he sent off a guard at once with orders to bring John's head. The guard left, went to the prison, and cut John's head off; then he brought it on a plate and gave it to the girl, who gave it to her mother. When John's disciples heard about this, they came and got his body, and buried it. (Mark 6:14–29)

# Reflections and Questions

## About the Reading

In the middle of the storm, Jesus asks, "Where is your faith?" because the disciples are afraid. It is also a calling for us to have courage. Once again it is a mob of evil spirits that declare that Jesus is the Son of the Most High God. The person who was possessed is now called to announce the wonders of God.

It is noteworthy that this woman, who has great faith, is determined to touch the cloak of Jesus. Her actions are in direct contrast to fear and cowardice. Jesus goes to the synagogue leader's house. His daughter was sick; now she is dead. The creator of life calls her to another purpose: "Get up." This is an order that comes from Jesus.

The harvest is large, but there are few workers to gather it in. This statement from Jesus is about his kingdom and those who dedicate themselves to preaching his message. They go like sheep amongst wolves. Evangelism is not about human triumphs; we see this chapter end with King Herod beheading Jesus' forerunner.

## Let's Meditate

God has a mission for each of us.

- Jesus once again asks you in the midst of your storms, "Where is your faith?" How do you respond to Jesus?
- No matter how bad things are going, if you accept the Lord and his healing, you, too, can become a missionary disciple. How can you remind yourself of this truth during a hard time?
- How can you relate to the woman who, in her weakness and illness, touched Jesus' cloak? When has it been a struggle for you to reach out for Jesus' healing?
- For Jesus, even death is not an obstacle. Can you also hear the Lord's call to "get up"? Can you make a list of all the things that keep you down—and take that list to the Lord?
- Does the phrase *there are few workers* challenge you? Jesus himself makes his word relevant for today by calling you.

## Ask God

Take some time for quiet reflection. In your own words, ask God to show you, through this Gospel reading, a clear path to the calling he has revealed to you.

## Think about the Main Idea

Look for the phrase in the reading that most catches your attention, and repeat it to yourself several times. You might also write it in a journal so that you can revisit it and think about it again.

## Create an Action Plan

Reading the Bible and praying with it can move us to change.

- How can this reading help you understand your calling better?
- What concrete action can you take to bring your prayer and meditation into daily life?

## Discussion Questions

1. Jesus calms a raging storm by ordering the wind to stop and commanding the waves to be calm. How are Jesus' words relevant to the storms you face: your emotions, circumstances, and relationships?

2. Before Jesus sends out his twelve disciples to proclaim God's kingdom and heal the sick, he describes the harvest as "large" and its workers as "few." Would you say that this remains true today, or not? What makes you think that?

3. Jesus warns that "those who do not take up their cross and follow in my steps are not fit to be my disciples. Those who try to gain their own life will lose it; but those who lose their life for my sake will gain it." What do you think you would "gain" if you followed Jesus? What do you think you might "lose"? What—if anything—makes the trade-off worth it?

# 9

# Feeding the Hungry Crowds

The apostles returned and met with Jesus, and told him all they had done and taught. There were so many people coming and going that Jesus and his disciples didn't even have time to eat. So he said to them, "Let us go off by ourselves to some place where we will be alone and you can rest a while." So they started out in a boat by themselves to a lonely place.

Many people, however, saw them leave and knew at once who they were; so they went from all the towns and ran ahead by land and arrived at the place ahead of Jesus and his disciples. When Jesus got out of the boat, he saw this large crowd, and his heart was filled with pity for them, because they were like sheep without a shepherd. So he began to teach them many things. (Mark 6:30–34)

That evening his disciples came to him and said, "It is already very late, and this is a lonely place. Send the people away and let them go to the villages to buy food for themselves."

"They don't have to leave," answered Jesus. "You yourselves give them something to eat!" (Matthew 14:15–16)

Jesus looked around and saw that a large crowd was coming to him, so he asked Philip, "Where can we buy enough food to feed all these people?" (He said this to test Philip; actually he already knew what he would do.)

Philip answered, "For everyone to have even a little, it would take more than two hundred silver coins to buy enough bread."

Another one of his disciples, Andrew, who was Simon Peter's brother, said, "There is a boy here who has five loaves of barley bread and two fish. But they will certainly not be enough for all these people."

"Make the people sit down," Jesus told them. (There was a lot of grass there.) So all the people sat down; there were about five thousand men. Jesus took the bread, gave thanks to God, and distributed it to the people who were sitting there. He did the same with the fish, and they all had as much as they wanted. When they were all full, he said to his disciples, "Gather the pieces left over; let us not waste a bit." So they gathered them all and filled twelve baskets with the pieces left over from the five barley loaves which the people had eaten.

Seeing this miracle that Jesus had performed, the people there said, "Surely this is the Prophet who was to come into the world!" (John 6:5–14)

Then Jesus made the disciples get into the boat and go on ahead to the other side of the lake, while he sent the people away. After sending the people away, he went up a hill by himself to pray.

When evening came, Jesus was there alone; and by this time the boat was far out in the lake, tossed about by the waves, because the wind was blowing against it.

Between three and six o'clock in the morning Jesus came to the disciples, walking on the water. When they saw him walking on the water, they were terrified. "It's a ghost!" they said, and screamed with fear.

Jesus spoke to them at once. "Courage!" he said. "It is I. Don't be afraid!"

Then Peter spoke up. "Lord, if it is really you, order me to come out on the water to you."

"Come!" answered Jesus. So Peter got out of the boat and started walking on the water to Jesus. But when he noticed the strong wind, he was afraid and started to sink down in the water. "Save me, Lord!" he cried.

At once Jesus reached out and grabbed hold of him and said, "What little faith you have! Why did you doubt?"

They both got into the boat, and the wind died down. Then the disciples in the boat worshiped Jesus. "Truly you are the Son of God!" they exclaimed.

They crossed the lake and came to land at Gennesaret, where the people recognized Jesus. So they sent for the sick people in all the surrounding country and brought them to Jesus. They begged him to let the sick at least touch the edge of his cloak; and all who touched it were made well. (Matthew 14:22–36)

Next day the crowd which had stayed on the other side of the lake realized that there had been only one boat there. They knew that Jesus had not gone in it with his disciples, but that they had left without him. Other boats, which were from Tiberias, came to shore near the place where the crowd had eaten the bread after the Lord had given thanks. When the crowd saw that Jesus was not there, nor his disciples, they got into those boats and went to Capernaum, looking for him.

When the people found Jesus on the other side of the lake, they said to him, "Teacher, when did you get here?"

Jesus answered, "I am telling you the truth: you are looking for me because you ate the bread and had all you wanted, not because you understood my miracles. Do not work for food that spoils; instead, work for the food that lasts for eternal life. This is the food which the Son of Man will give you, because God, the Father, has put his mark of approval on him."

So they asked him, "What can we do in order to do what God wants us to do?"

Jesus answered, "What God wants you to do is to believe in the one he sent."

They replied, "What miracle will you perform so that we may see it and believe you? What will you do? Our ancestors ate manna in the desert, just as the scripture says, 'He gave them bread from heaven to eat.'"

"I am telling you the truth," Jesus said. "What Moses gave you was not the bread from heaven; it is my Father who gives you the real bread from heaven. For the bread that God gives is he who comes down from heaven and gives life to the world."

"Sir," they asked him, "give us this bread always."

"I am the bread of life," Jesus told them. "Those who come to me will never be hungry; those who believe in me will never be thirsty. Now, I told you that you have seen me but will not believe. Everyone whom my Father gives me will come to me. I will never turn away anyone who comes to me, because I have come down from heaven to do not my own will but the will of him who sent me. And it is the will of him who sent me that I should not lose any of all those he has given me, but that I should raise them all to life on the last day. For what my Father wants is that all who see the Son and believe in him should have eternal life. And I will raise them to life on the last day."

The people started grumbling about him, because he said, "I am the bread that came down from heaven." So they said, "This man is Jesus son of Joseph, isn't he? We know his father and mother. How, then, does he now say he came down from heaven?"

Jesus answered, "Stop grumbling among yourselves. People cannot come to me unless the Father who sent me draws them to me; and I will raise them to life on the last day. The prophets wrote, 'Everyone will be taught by God.' Anyone who hears the Father and learns from him comes to me. This does not mean that anyone has seen the Father; he who is from God is the only one who has seen the Father. I am telling you the truth: he who believes has eternal life. I am the bread of life. Your ancestors ate manna in the desert, but they died. But the bread that comes down from heaven is of such a kind that whoever eats it will not die. I am the living bread that came down from heaven. If you eat this bread, you will live forever. The bread that I will give you is my flesh, which I give so that the world may live."

This started an angry argument among them. "How can this man give us his flesh to eat?" they asked.

Jesus said to them, "I am telling you the truth: if you do not eat the flesh of the Son of Man and drink his blood, you will not have life in yourselves. Those who eat my flesh and drink my blood have eternal life, and I will raise them to life on the last day. For my flesh is the real food; my blood is the real drink. Those who eat my flesh and drink my blood live in me, and I live in them. The living Father sent me, and because of him I live also. In the same way whoever eats me will live because of me. This, then, is the bread that came down from heaven; it is not like the bread that your ancestors ate, but then later died. Those who eat this bread will live forever."

Jesus said this as he taught in the synagogue in Capernaum.

Many of his followers heard this and said, "This teaching is too hard. Who can listen to it?" Without being told, Jesus knew that they were grumbling about this, so he said to them, "Does this make you want to give up? Suppose, then, that you should see the Son of Man go back up to the place where he was before? What gives life is God's Spirit; human power is of no use at all. The words I have spoken to you bring God's life-giving Spirit. Yet some of you do not believe." (Jesus knew from the very beginning who were the ones that would not believe and which one would betray him.) And he added, "This is the very reason I told you that no people can come to me unless the Father makes it possible for them to do so."

Because of this, many of Jesus' followers turned back and would not go with him any more. So he asked the twelve disciples, "And you—would you also like to leave?"

Simon Peter answered him, "Lord, to whom would we go? You have the words that give eternal life. And now we believe and know that you are the Holy One who has come from God."

Jesus replied, "I chose the twelve of you, didn't I? Yet one of you is a devil!" He was talking about Judas, the son of Simon Iscariot. For Judas, even though he was one of the twelve disciples, was going to betray him. (John 6:22–71)

Some Pharisees and teachers of the Law who had come from Jerusalem gathered around Jesus. They noticed that some of his disciples were eating their food with hands that were ritually unclean—that is, they had not washed them in the way the Pharisees said people should. (For the Pharisees, as well as the rest of the Jews, follow the teaching they received from their ancestors: they do not eat unless they wash their hands in the proper way; nor do they eat anything that comes from the market unless they wash it first. And they follow many other rules which they have received, such as the proper way to wash cups, pots, copper bowls, and beds.)

So the Pharisees and the teachers of the Law asked Jesus, "Why is it that your disciples do not follow the teaching handed down by our ancestors, but instead eat with ritually unclean hands?"

Jesus answered them, "How right Isaiah was when he prophesied about you! You are hypocrites, just as he wrote: 'These people, says God, honor me with their words, but their heart is really far away from me. It is no use for them to worship me, because they teach human rules as though they were my laws!' You put aside God's command and obey human teachings."

And Jesus continued, "You have a clever way of rejecting God's law in order to uphold your own teaching. For Moses commanded, 'Respect your father and your mother,' and, 'If you curse your father or your mother, you are to be put to death.' But you teach that if people have something they could use to help their father or mother, but say, 'This is Corban' (which means, "it belongs to God"), they are excused from helping their father or mother. In this way the teaching you pass on to others cancels out the word of God. And there are many other things like this that you do."

Then Jesus called the crowd to him once more and said to them, "Listen to me, all of you, and understand. There is nothing that goes into you from the outside which can make you ritually unclean. Rather, it is what comes out of you that makes you unclean. Listen then if you have ears!" (Mark 7:1–16)

Then the disciples came to him and said, "Do you know that the Pharisees had their feelings hurt by what you said?"

"Every plant which my Father in heaven did not plant will be pulled up," answered Jesus. "Don't worry about them! They are blind leaders of the blind; and when one blind man leads another, both fall into a ditch."

Peter spoke up, "Explain this saying to us."

Jesus said to them, "You are still no more intelligent than the others. Don't you understand? Anything that goes into your mouth goes into your stomach and then on out of your body. But the things that come out of the mouth come from the heart, and these are the things that make you ritually unclean.

For from your heart come the evil ideas which lead you to kill, commit adultery, and do other immoral things; to rob, lie, and slander others. These are the things that make you unclean. But to eat without washing your hands as they say you should—this doesn't make you unclean."

Jesus left that place and went off to the territory near the cities of Tyre and Sidon. A Canaanite woman who lived in that region came to him. "Son of David!" she cried out. "Have mercy on me, sir! My daughter has a demon and is in a terrible condition."

But Jesus did not say a word to her. His disciples came to him and begged him, "Send her away! She is following us and making all this noise!"

Then Jesus replied, "I have been sent only to the lost sheep of the people of Israel."

At this the woman came and fell at his feet. "Help me, sir!" she said.

Jesus answered, "It isn't right to take the children's food and throw it to the dogs."

"That's true, sir," she answered, "but even the dogs eat the leftovers that fall from their masters' table."

So Jesus answered her, "You are a woman of great faith! What you want will be done for you." And at that very moment her daughter was healed. (Matthew 15:12–28)

Jesus then left the neighborhood of Tyre and went on through Sidon to Lake Galilee, going by way of the territory of the Ten Towns. Some people brought him a man who was deaf and could hardly speak, and they begged Jesus to place his hands on him. So Jesus took him off alone, away from the crowd, put his fingers in the man's ears, spat, and touched the man's tongue. Then Jesus looked up to heaven, gave a deep groan, and said to the man, "*Ephphatha*," which means, "Open up!"

At once the man was able to hear, his speech impediment was removed, and he began to talk without any trouble. Then Jesus ordered the people not to speak of it to anyone; but the more he ordered them not to, the more they told it. And all who heard were completely amazed. "How well he does everything!" they exclaimed. "He even causes the deaf to hear and the dumb to speak!" (Mark 7:31–37)

Jesus called his disciples to him and said, "I feel sorry for these people, because they have been with me for three days and now have nothing to eat. I don't want to send them away without feeding them, for they might faint on their way home."

The disciples asked him, "Where will we find enough food in this desert to feed this crowd?"

"How much bread do you have?" Jesus asked.

"Seven loaves," they answered, "and a few small fish."

So Jesus ordered the crowd to sit down on the ground. Then he took the seven loaves and the fish, gave thanks to God, broke them, and gave them to the disciples; and the disciples gave them to the people. They all ate and had enough. Then the disciples took up seven baskets full of pieces left over. The number of men who ate was four thousand, not counting the women and children.

Then Jesus sent the people away, got into a boat, and went to the territory of Magadan. (Matthew 15:32–39)

Some Pharisees and Sadducees who came to Jesus wanted to trap him, so they asked him to perform a miracle for them, to show that God approved of him. But Jesus answered, "When the sun is setting, you say, 'We are going to have fine weather, because the sky is red.' And early in the morning you say, 'It is going to rain, because the sky is red and dark.' You can predict the weather by looking at the sky, but you cannot interpret the signs concerning these times! How evil and godless are the people of this day! You ask me for a miracle? No! The only miracle you will be given is the miracle of Jonah."

So he left them and went away.

When the disciples crossed over to the other side of the lake, they forgot to take any bread. Jesus said to them, "Take care; be on your guard against the yeast of the Pharisees and Sadducees."

They started discussing among themselves, "He says this because we didn't bring any bread."

Jesus knew what they were saying, so he asked them, "Why are you discussing among yourselves about not having any bread? What little faith you have! Don't you understand yet? Don't you remember when I broke the five loaves for the five thousand men? How many baskets did you fill? And what about the seven loaves for the four thousand men? How many baskets did you fill? How is it that you don't understand that I was not talking to you about bread? Guard yourselves from the yeast of the Pharisees and Sadducees!"

Then the disciples understood that he was not warning them to guard themselves from the yeast used in bread but from the teaching of the Pharisees and Sadducees. (Matthew 16:1–12)

# Reflections and Questions

## About the Reading

Notice Jesus' instructions: "Give them something to eat." He did not send them to buy food but had faith it would be provided. Afterward, he went off by himself to pray.

The disciples were in a boat at night being tossed about by the waves. When they saw Jesus walking on the water they were terrified. But he assured them, "Do not be afraid"—an encouragement repeated many times in the Bible. Jesus called Peter to come to him. It is challenging to be called to go to the Lord in the middle of a raging sea. When Peter took his eyes off Jesus, he started to sink, and Jesus spoke to him, "What little faith you have! Why did you doubt?"

The work of God encourages our belief in Jesus. He is the bread of life; whoever feeds on him will have eternal life. This teaching was very difficult for some. Jesus, understanding their hearts, asked his disciples, "And you—would you also like to leave?" Peter replied, "Lord, to whom would we go? You have the words that give eternal life."

## Let's Meditate

God has a mission for each of us.

- In what way is feeding the hungry part of your calling and mission as a Christian?
- In times of hardship, do you hear the Lord telling you, "Do not be afraid"? At those times, how much are you listening for Jesus' voice?
- Even if you find yourself in a stormy sea, Jesus calls to you. You know that if you take your eyes away from him, you sink. Do you have the courage to say, "Save me, Lord"? Do you hear Jesus reproaching your lack of faith?
- If vocation and calling are about believing, how do you see your own faith? What, if anything, is missing?
- Could you say with courage, "Lord, to whom would I go? You have the words that give eternal life"? How does that apply to your personal life?

**Ask God**

Take some time for quiet reflection. In your own words, ask God to show you, through this Gospel reading, a clear path to the calling he has revealed to you.

**Think about the Main Idea**

Look for the phrase in the reading that most catches your attention, and repeat it to yourself several times. You might also write it in a journal so that you can revisit it and think about it again.

**Create an Action Plan**

Reading the Bible and praying with it can move us to change.

- How can this reading help you understand your calling better?
- What concrete action can you take to bring your prayer and meditation into daily life?

**Discussion Questions**

1. On two different occasions, Jesus takes a few loaves of bread and feeds thousands of people. What motivates Jesus to do this? What does this say about Jesus' care for people's needs? What does it say about Jesus' care for you?

2. When Jesus beckons Peter to come to him on the water, what do you admire about Peter's actions and attitudes? What did he do that Jesus didn't like? Is Jesus perhaps inviting you to leave the safety of a "boat" in your life and walk out toward him?

3. Jesus warns that just as a tiny amount of yeast can affect a large amount of dough, the evil tendencies of the Pharisees and Sadducees can greatly pollute their surroundings. What do you think Jesus found so appalling about the actions and attitudes of these religious leaders?

# 10

# Seen in God's Glory

They came to Bethsaida, where some people brought a blind man to Jesus and begged him to touch him. Jesus took the blind man by the hand and led him out of the village. After spitting on the man's eyes, Jesus placed his hands on him and asked him, "Can you see anything?"

The man looked up and said, "Yes, I can see people, but they look like trees walking around."

Jesus again placed his hands on the man's eyes. This time the man looked intently, his eyesight returned, and he saw everything clearly. Jesus then sent him home with the order, "Don't go back into the village."

Then Jesus and his disciples went away to the villages near Caesarea Philippi. On the way he asked them, "Tell me, who do people say I am?"

"Some say that you are John the Baptist," they answered; "others say that you are Elijah, while others say that you are one of the prophets." (Mark 8:22–28)

"What about you?" he asked them. "Who do you say I am?"

Simon Peter answered, "You are the Messiah, the Son of the living God."

"Good for you, Simon son of John!" answered Jesus. "For this truth did not come to you from any human being, but it was given to you directly by my Father in heaven. And so I tell you, Peter: you are a rock, and on this rock foundation I will build my church, and not even death will ever be able to overcome it. I will give you the keys of the Kingdom of heaven; what you prohibit on earth will be prohibited in heaven, and what you permit on earth will be permitted in heaven."

Then Jesus ordered his disciples not to tell anyone that he was the Messiah.

From that time on Jesus began to say plainly to his disciples, "I must go to Jerusalem and suffer much from the elders, the chief priests, and the teachers of the Law. I will be put to death, but three days later I will be raised to life."

Peter took him aside and began to rebuke him. "God forbid it, Lord!" he said. "That must never happen to you!"

Jesus turned around and said to Peter, "Get away from me, Satan! You are an obstacle in my way, because these thoughts of yours don't come from God, but from human nature."

Then Jesus said to his disciples, "If any of you want to come with me, you must forget yourself, carry your cross, and follow me. For if you want to save your own life, you will lose it; but if you lose your life for my sake, you will find it. Will you gain anything if you win the whole world but lose your life? Of course not! There is nothing you can give to regain your life. For the Son of Man is about to come in the glory of his Father with his angels, and then he will reward each one according to his deeds. I assure you that there are some here who will not die until they have seen the Son of Man come as King." (Matthew 16:15–28)

About a week after he had said these things, Jesus took Peter, John, and James with him and went up a hill to pray. While he was praying, his face changed its appearance, and his clothes became dazzling white. Suddenly two men were there talking with him. They were Moses and Elijah, who appeared in heavenly glory and talked with Jesus about the way in which he would soon fulfill God's purpose by dying in Jerusalem. Peter and his companions were sound asleep, but they woke up and saw Jesus' glory and the two men who were standing with him. (Luke 9:28–32)

So Peter spoke up and said to Jesus, "Lord, how good it is that we are here! If you wish, I will make three tents here, one for you, one for Moses, and one for Elijah."

While he was talking, a shining cloud came over them, and a voice from the cloud said, "This is my own dear Son, with whom I am pleased—listen to him!"

When the disciples heard the voice, they were so terrified that they threw themselves face downward on the ground. Jesus came to them and touched them. "Get up," he said. "Don't be afraid!" So they looked up and saw no one there but Jesus.

As they came down the mountain, Jesus ordered them, "Don't tell anyone about this vision you have seen until the Son of Man has been raised from death."

Then the disciples asked Jesus, "Why do the teachers of the Law say that Elijah has to come first?"

"Elijah is indeed coming first," answered Jesus, "and he will get everything ready. But I tell you that Elijah has already come and people did not recognize him, but treated him just as they pleased. In the same way they will also mistreat the Son of Man."

Then the disciples understood that he was talking to them about John the Baptist. (Matthew 17:4–13)

When they joined the rest of the disciples, they saw a large crowd around them and some teachers of the Law arguing with them. When the people saw Jesus, they were greatly surprised, and ran to him and greeted him. Jesus asked his disciples, "What are you arguing with them about?"

A man in the crowd answered, "Teacher, I brought my son to you, because he has an evil spirit in him and cannot talk. Whenever the spirit attacks him, it throws him to the ground, and he foams at the mouth, grits his teeth, and becomes stiff all over. I asked your disciples to drive the spirit out, but they could not."

Jesus said to them, "How unbelieving you people are! How long must I stay with you? How long do I have to put up with you? Bring the boy to me!" They brought him to Jesus.

As soon as the spirit saw Jesus, it threw the boy into a fit, so that he fell on the ground and rolled around, foaming at the mouth. "How long has he been like this?" Jesus asked the father.

"Ever since he was a child," he replied. "Many times the evil spirit has tried to kill him by throwing him in the fire and into water. Have pity on us and help us, if you possibly can!"

"Yes," said Jesus, "if you yourself can! Everything is possible for the person who has faith."

The father at once cried out, "I do have faith, but not enough. Help me have more!"

Jesus noticed that the crowd was closing in on them, so he gave a command to the evil spirit. "Deaf and dumb spirit," he said, "I order you to come out of the boy and never go into him again!"

The spirit screamed, threw the boy into a bad fit, and came out. The boy looked like a corpse, and everyone said, "He is dead!" But Jesus took the boy by the hand and helped him rise, and he stood up.

After Jesus had gone indoors, his disciples asked him privately, "Why couldn't we drive the spirit out?"

"Only prayer can drive this kind out," answered Jesus; "nothing else can."

Jesus and his disciples left that place and went on through Galilee. Jesus did not want anyone to know where he was, because he was teaching his disciples: "The Son of Man will be handed over to those who will kill him. Three days later, however, he will rise to life."

But they did not understand what this teaching meant, and they were afraid to ask him. (Mark 9:14–32)

When Jesus and his disciples came to Capernaum, the collectors of the Temple tax came to Peter and asked, "Does your teacher pay the Temple tax?"

"Of course," Peter answered.

When Peter went into the house, Jesus spoke up first, "Simon, what is your opinion? Who pays duties or taxes to the kings of this world? The citizens of the country or the foreigners?"

"The foreigners," answered Peter.

"Well, then," replied Jesus, "that means that the citizens don't have to pay. But we don't want to offend these people. So go to the lake and drop in a line. Pull up the first fish you hook, and in its mouth you will find a coin worth enough for my Temple tax and yours. Take it and pay them our taxes." (Matthew 17:24–27)

At that time the disciples came to Jesus, asking, "Who is the greatest in the Kingdom of heaven?"

So Jesus called a child to come and stand in front of them, and said, "I assure you that unless you change and become like children, you will never enter the Kingdom of heaven. The greatest in the Kingdom of heaven is the one who humbles himself and becomes like this child. And whoever welcomes in my name one such child as this, welcomes me." (Matthew 18:1–5)

John said to him, "Teacher, we saw a man who was driving out demons in your name, and we told him to stop, because he doesn't belong to our group."

"Do not try to stop him," Jesus told them, "because no one who performs a miracle in my name will be able soon afterward to say evil things about me. For whoever is not against us is for us. I assure you that anyone who gives you a drink of water because you belong to me will certainly receive a reward.

"If anyone should cause one of these little ones to lose faith in me, it would be better for that person to have a large millstone tied around the neck and be thrown into the sea. So if your hand makes you lose your faith, cut it off! It is better for you to enter life without a hand than to keep both hands and go off to hell, to the fire that never goes out. And if your foot makes you lose your faith, cut it off! It is better for you to enter life without a foot than to keep both feet and be thrown into hell. And if your eye makes you lose your faith, take it out! It is better for you to enter the Kingdom of God with only one eye than to keep both eyes and be thrown into hell. There 'the worms that eat them never die, and the fire that burns them is never put out.'

"Everyone will be purified by fire as a sacrifice is purified by salt.

"Salt is good; but if it loses its saltiness, how can you make it salty again?

"Have the salt of friendship among yourselves, and live in peace with one another. (Mark 9:38–50)

"See that you don't despise any of these little ones. Their angels in heaven, I tell you, are always in the presence of my Father in heaven.

"What do you think a man does who has one hundred sheep and one of them gets lost? He will leave the other ninety-nine grazing on the hillside and go and look for the lost sheep. When he finds it, I tell you, he feels far happier over this one sheep than over the ninety-nine that did not get lost. In just the same way your Father in heaven does not want any of these little ones to be lost.

"If your brother sins against you, go to him and show him his fault. But do it privately, just between yourselves. If he listens to you, you have won your brother back. But if he will not listen to you, take one or two other persons with you, so that 'every accusation may be upheld by the testimony of two or more witnesses,' as the scripture says. And if he will not listen to them, then tell the whole thing to the church. Finally, if he will not listen to the church, treat him as though he were a pagan or a tax collector.

"And so I tell all of you: what you prohibit on earth will be prohibited in heaven, and what you permit on earth will be permitted in heaven.

"And I tell you more: whenever two of you on earth agree about anything you pray for, it will be done for you by my Father in heaven. For where two or three come together in my name, I am there with them."

Then Peter came to Jesus and asked, "Lord, if my brother keeps on sinning against me, how many times do I have to forgive him? Seven times?"

"No, not seven times," answered Jesus, "but seventy times seven, because the Kingdom of heaven is like this. Once there was a king who decided to check on his servants' accounts. He had just begun to do so when one of them was brought in who owed him millions of dollars. The servant did not have enough to pay his debt, so the king ordered him to be sold as a slave, with his wife and his children and all that he had, in order to pay the debt. The servant fell on his knees before the king. 'Be patient with me,' he begged, 'and

I will pay you everything!' The king felt sorry for him, so he forgave him the debt and let him go.

"Then the man went out and met one of his fellow servants who owed him a few dollars. He grabbed him and started choking him. 'Pay back what you owe me!' he said. His fellow servant fell down and begged him, 'Be patient with me, and I will pay you back!' But he refused; instead, he had him thrown into jail until he should pay the debt. When the other servants saw what had happened, they were very upset and went to the king and told him every-thing. So he called the servant in. 'You worthless slave!' he said. 'I forgave you the whole amount you owed me, just because you asked me to. You should have had mercy on your fellow servant, just as I had mercy on you.' The king was very angry, and he sent the servant to jail to be punished until he should pay back the whole amount."

And Jesus concluded, "That is how my Father in heaven will treat every one of you unless you forgive your brother from your heart." (Matthew 18:10–35)

# Reflections and Questions

## About the Reading

After giving sight to the blind man, because the people were arguing about it, Jesus asked: "Who do people say I am?" Simon Peter replied, "You are the Messiah, the Son of the living God." Although he recognized the Messiah, he tried to prevent Jesus from going to Jerusalem to suffer. "Get away from me, Satan!" was Jesus' harsh reaction.

Whoever wants to follow Jesus must deny himself, carry his cross, and make a commitment to follow him. This is perhaps the most important calling for a disciple.

The Father declares at the moment of the Transfiguration, "This is my own dear Son, listen to him!" Again, we are called to listen to Jesus.

The first call is to believe; the next is to spread the faith. Our witness should be given first and foremost through love and forgiveness.

## Let's Meditate

God has a mission for each of us.

- If we did a survey about Jesus today, what do you think people would say? What would you say about Jesus?

- Even when we recognize Jesus, we can obstruct him from revealing himself in many different ways. One person who was putting up obstacles he called "Satan." Could it be that our behavior can hinder Jesus' plan for the salvation of all? Could it be that Jesus also says that to us?

- The call to follow Jesus implies a denial of self. Are you willing to look closely at yourself and do everything to abandon what prevents you from being a faithful witness of Jesus' love—such as pride, selfishness, ambition, and so on?

- In what ways do you "listen"—that is, obey and follow Jesus, as the Father has asked you to do?

**Ask God**

Take some time for quiet reflection. In your own words, ask God to show you, through this Gospel reading, a clear path to the calling he has revealed to you.

**Think about the Main Idea**

Look for the phrase in the reading that most catches your attention, and repeat it to yourself several times. You might also write it in a journal so that you can revisit it and think about it again.

**Create an Action Plan**

Reading the Bible and praying with it can move us to change.

- How can this reading help you understand your calling better?
- What concrete action can you take to bring your prayer and meditation into daily life?

**Discussion Questions**

1. As Jesus walks with his disciples to the villages around Caesarea Philippi, he asks them two key questions: "Who do people say I am?" and "Who do you say that I am?" How would people you know answer those two questions about Jesus? How would you answer those two questions?

2. The father of a boy controlled by an evil spirit cries out, "I do have faith, but not enough, help me have more." In short, he lets Jesus know that he does believe in him, and yet there are parts of his faith that need help. In what ways is your faith already strong? Where do you need help ?

3. In the midst of a first-century culture that didn't always treasure children, Jesus tells his disciples that they need to "welcome" little children and "become like little children." What is it about children that Jesus found so powerful?

# 11

# Claiming God's Name

After this, Jesus traveled in Galilee; he did not want to travel in Judea, because the Jewish authorities there were wanting to kill him. The time for the Festival of Shelters was near, so Jesus' brothers said to him, "Leave this place and go to Judea, so that your followers will see the things that you are doing. People don't hide what they are doing if they want to be well known. Since you are doing these things, let the whole world know about you!"

Not even his brothers believed in him.

Jesus said to them, "The right time for me has not yet come. Any time is right for you. The world cannot hate you, but it hates me, because I keep telling it that its ways are bad. You go on to the festival. I am not going to this festival, because the right time has not come for me." He said this and then stayed on in Galilee.

After his brothers had gone to the festival, Jesus also went; however, he did not go openly, but secretly. (John 7:1–10)

As the time drew near when Jesus would be taken up to heaven, he made up his mind and set out on his way to Jerusalem. He sent messengers ahead of him, who went into a village in Samaria to get everything ready for him. But the people there would not receive him, because it was clear that he was on his way to Jerusalem. When the disciples James and John saw this, they said, "Lord, do you want us to call fire down from heaven to destroy them?"

Jesus turned and rebuked them. Then Jesus and his disciples went on to another village.

As they went on their way, a man said to Jesus, "I will follow you wherever you go."

Jesus said to him, "Foxes have holes, and birds have nests, but the Son of Man has no place to lie down and rest."

He said to another man, "Follow me."

But that man said, "Sir, first let me go back and bury my father."

Jesus answered, "Let the dead bury their own dead. You go and proclaim the Kingdom of God."

Someone else said, "I will follow you, sir; but first let me go and say good-bye to my family."

Jesus said to him, "Anyone who starts to plow and then keeps looking back is of no use for the Kingdom of God." (Luke 9:51–62)

The Jewish authorities were looking for him at the festival. "Where is he?" they asked.

There was much whispering about him in the crowd. "He is a good man," some people said. "No," others said, "he fools the people." But no one talked about him openly, because they were afraid of the Jewish authorities.

The festival was nearly half over when Jesus went to the Temple and began teaching. The Jewish authorities were greatly surprised and said, "How does this man know so much when he has never been to school?"

Jesus answered, "What I teach is not my own teaching, but it comes from God, who sent me. Whoever is willing to do what God wants will know whether what I teach comes from God or whether I speak on my own authority. Those who speak on their own authority are trying to gain glory for themselves. But he who wants glory for the one who sent him is honest, and there is nothing false in him. Moses gave you the Law, didn't he? But not one of you obeys the Law. Why are you trying to kill me?"

"You have a demon in you!" the crowd answered. "Who is trying to kill you?"

Jesus answered, "I performed one miracle, and you were all surprised. Moses ordered you to circumcise your sons (although it was not Moses but your ancestors who started it), and so you circumcise a boy on the Sabbath. If a boy is circumcised on the Sabbath so that Moses' Law is not broken, why are you angry with me because I made a man completely well on the Sabbath? Stop judging by external standards, and judge by true standards."

Some of the people of Jerusalem said, "Isn't this the man the authorities are trying to kill? Look! He is talking in public, and they say nothing against him! Can it be that they really know that he is the Messiah? But when the Messiah comes, no one will know where he is from. And we all know where this man comes from."

As Jesus taught in the Temple, he said in a loud voice, "Do you really know me and know where I am from? I have not come on my own authority. He who sent me, however, is truthful. You do not know him, but I know him, because I come from him and he sent me."

Then they tried to seize him, but no one laid a hand on him, because his hour had not yet come. But many in the crowd believed in him and said, "When the Messiah comes, will he perform more miracles than this man has?"

The Pharisees heard the crowd whispering these things about Jesus, so they and the chief priests sent some guards to arrest him. Jesus said, "I shall be with you a little while longer, and then I shall go away to him who sent me. You will look for me, but you will not find me, because you cannot go where I will be."

The Jewish authorities said among themselves, "Where is he about to go so that we shall not find him? Will he go to the Greek cities where our people live, and teach the Greeks? He says that we will look for him but will not find him, and that we cannot go where he will be. What does he mean?"

On the last and most important day of the festival Jesus stood up and said in a loud voice, "Whoever is thirsty should come to me, and whoever believes in me should drink. As the scripture says, 'Streams of life-giving water will pour out from his side.'" Jesus said this about the Spirit, which those who believed in him were going to receive. At that time the Spirit had not yet been given, because Jesus had not been raised to glory.

Some of the people in the crowd heard him say this and said, "This man is really the Prophet!"

Others said, "He is the Messiah!"

But others said, "The Messiah will not come from Galilee! The scripture says that the Messiah will be a descendant of King David and will be born in Bethlehem, the town where David lived."

So there was a division in the crowd because of Jesus. Some wanted to seize him, but no one laid a hand on him.

When the guards went back, the chief priests and Pharisees asked them, "Why did you not bring him?"

The guards answered, "Nobody has ever talked the way this man does!"

"Did he fool you, too?" the Pharisees asked them. "Have you ever known one of the authorities or one Pharisee to believe in him? This crowd does not know the Law of Moses, so they are under God's curse!"

One of the Pharisees there was Nicodemus, the man who had gone to see Jesus before. He said to the others, "According to our Law we cannot condemn people before hearing them and finding out what they have done."

"Well," they answered, "are you also from Galilee? Study the Scriptures and you will learn that no prophet ever comes from Galilee." (John 7:11–52)

Then everyone went home, but Jesus went to the Mount of Olives.

Early the next morning he went back to the Temple. All the people gathered around him, and he sat down and began to teach them. The teachers of the Law and the Pharisees brought in a woman who had been caught committing adultery, and they made her stand before them all. "Teacher," they said to Jesus, "this woman was caught in the very act of committing adultery. In our Law Moses commanded that such a woman must be stoned to death. Now, what do you say?" They said this to trap Jesus, so that they could accuse him. But he bent over and wrote on the ground with his finger. As they stood there asking him questions, he straightened up and said to them, "Whichever one of you has committed no sin may throw the first stone at her." Then he bent over again and wrote on the ground. When they heard this, they all left, one by one, the older ones first. Jesus was left alone, with the woman still standing there. He straightened up and said to her, "Where are they? Is there no one left to condemn you?"

"No one, sir," she answered.

"Well, then," Jesus said, "I do not condemn you either. Go, but do not sin again."

Jesus spoke to the Pharisees again. "I am the light of the world," he said. "Whoever follows me will have the light of life and will never walk in darkness."

The Pharisees said to him, "Now you are testifying on your own behalf; what you say proves nothing."

"No," Jesus answered, "even though I do testify on my own behalf, what I say is true, because I know where I came from and where I am going. You do not know where I came from or where I am going. You make judgments in a purely human way; I pass judgment on no one. But if I were to do so, my judgment would be true, because I am not alone in this; the Father who sent me is with me. It is written in your Law that when two witnesses agree, what they say is true. I testify on my own behalf, and the Father who sent me also testifies on my behalf."

"Where is your father?" they asked him.

"You know neither me nor my Father," Jesus answered. "If you knew me, you would know my Father also."

Jesus said all this as he taught in the Temple, in the room where the offering boxes were placed. And no one arrested him, because his hour had not come.

Again Jesus said to them, "I will go away; you will look for me, but you will die in your sins. You cannot go where I am going."

So the Jewish authorities said, "He says that we cannot go where he is going. Does this mean that he will kill himself?"

Jesus answered, "You belong to this world here below, but I come from above. You are from this world, but I am not from this world. That is why I told you that you will die in your sins. And you will die in your sins if you do not believe that 'I Am Who I Am'."

"Who are you?" they asked him.

Jesus answered, "What I have told you from the very beginning. I have much to say about you, much to condemn you for. The one who sent me, however, is truthful, and I tell the world only what I have heard from him."

They did not understand that Jesus was talking to them about the Father. So he said to them, "When you lift up the Son of Man, you will know that 'I Am Who I Am'; then you will know that I do nothing on my own authority, but I say only what the Father has instructed me to say. And he who sent me is with me; he has not left me alone, because I always do what pleases him."

Many who heard Jesus say these things believed in him.

So Jesus said to those who believed in him, "If you obey my teaching, you are really my disciples; you will know the truth, and the truth will set you free."

"We are the descendants of Abraham," they answered, "and we have never been anybody's slaves. What do you mean, then, by saying, 'You will be free'?"

Jesus said to them, "I am telling you the truth: everyone who sins is a slave of sin. A slave does not belong to a family permanently, but a son belongs there forever. If the Son sets you free, then you will be really free. I know you are Abraham's descendants. Yet you are trying to kill me, because you will not accept my teaching. I talk about what my Father has shown me, but you do what your father has told you."

They answered him, "Our father is Abraham."

"If you really were Abraham's children," Jesus replied, "you would do the same things that he did. All I have ever done is to tell you the truth I heard from God, yet you are trying to kill me. Abraham did nothing like this! You are doing what your father did."

"God himself is the only Father we have," they answered, "and we are his true children."

Jesus said to them, "If God really were your Father, you would love me, because I came from God and now I am here. I did not come on my own authority, but he sent me. Why do you not understand what I say? It is because you cannot bear to listen to my message. You are the children of your father, the Devil, and you want to follow your father's desires. From the very beginning he was a murderer and has never been on the side of truth, because there is no truth in him. When he tells a lie, he is only doing what is natural to him, because he is a liar and the father of all lies. But I tell the truth, and that is why you do not believe me. Which one of you can prove that I am guilty of sin? If I tell the truth, then why do you not believe me? He who comes from God listens to God's words. You, however, are not from God, and that is why you will not listen."

They asked Jesus, "Were we not right in saying that you are a Samaritan and have a demon in you?"

"I have no demon," Jesus answered. "I honor my Father, but you dishonor me. I am not seeking honor for myself. But there is one who is seeking it and who judges in my favor. I am telling you the truth: whoever obeys my teaching will never die."

They said to him, "Now we know for sure that you have a demon! Abraham died, and the prophets died, yet you say that whoever obeys your teaching will never die. Our father Abraham died; you do not claim to be greater than Abraham, do you? And the prophets also died. Who do you think you are?"

Jesus answered, "If I were to honor myself, that honor would be worth nothing. The one who honors me is my Father—the very one you say is your God. You have never known him, but I know him. If I were to say that I do not know him, I would be a liar like you. But I do know him, and I obey his word. Your father Abraham rejoiced that he was to see the time of my coming; he saw it and was glad."

They said to him, "You are not even fifty years old—and you have seen Abraham?"

"I am telling you the truth," Jesus replied. "Before Abraham was born, 'I Am'."

Then they picked up stones to throw at him, but Jesus hid himself and left the Temple. (John 8:1–59)

# Reflections and Questions

### About the Reading

Notice how many people made excuses not to follow Jesus immediately: excuses such as taking care of their parents or family. His response is hard: "Anyone who starts to plow and then keeps looking back is of no use for the Kingdom of God."

Jesus was sent with a mission: the Father sent him to bear witness to the truth and thus save the world. We need to be willing to do what God wants.

Jesus came to save, not condemn. We see this clearly in the episode of the adulterous woman: "Whichever one of you has committed no sin may throw the first stone at her."

Walk in the light; this is a recurring theme. Jesus is the light of the world, and whoever is with him will have the light of life.

### Let's Meditate

God has a mission for each of us.

- Identify some obstacles that threaten to stop you from following Jesus. Have you ever used your past or your mistakes as an excuse not to follow the Lord?

- Think about the obedience of Jesus to the will of the Father that saves us. How do you testify to the truth when doing so might cause you problems?

- When you find someone in the wrong, are you more inclined to point to rules and regulations or to show mercy?

- When are you most tempted to "throw stones" at others for their wrongdoing? How can you follow Jesus' example when the rules of the church are at stake?

- Your vocation is to live in the light and to spread the light of Jesus in the midst of the darkness around us. How might you live the light today?

## Ask God

Take some time for quiet reflection. In your own words, ask God to show you, through this Gospel reading, a clear path to the calling he has revealed to you.

## Think about the Main Idea

Look for the phrase in the reading that most catches your attention, and repeat it to yourself several times. You might also write it in a journal so that you can revisit it and think about it again.

## Create an Action Plan

Reading the Bible and praying with it can move us to change.

- How can this reading help you understand your calling better?
- What concrete action can you take to bring your prayer and meditation into daily life?

## Discussion Questions

1. The religious leaders trap a woman caught in adultery in order to trap Jesus in a position where he has to choose between law and grace. How does his response turn the tables on this trap—for both the leaders and the woman?

2. Jesus explains to the Jews that his truth will set them free. What do you think they need freedom from? In what areas of your life would you like freedom? What might that look like?

3. Jesus describes the devil as the "father of all lies" who leads people to believe they are less than what God has intended for creation. What types of lies do you believe about yourself and our world? What truth can you keep in mind to respond to those lies in the future?

# 12

# Who Is He?

After this the Lord chose another seventy-two men and sent them out two by two, to go ahead of him to every town and place where he himself was about to go.

He said to them, "There is a large harvest, but few workers to gather it in. Pray to the owner of the harvest that he will send out workers to gather in his harvest. Go! I am sending you like lambs among wolves. Don't take a purse or a beggar's bag or shoes; don't stop to greet anyone on the road. Whenever you go into a house, first say, 'Peace be with this house.' If someone who is peace-loving lives there, let your greeting of peace remain on that person; if not, take back your greeting of peace. Stay in that same house, eating and drinking whatever they offer you, for workers should be given their pay. Don't move around from one house to another. Whenever you go into a town and are made welcome, eat what is set before you, heal the sick in that town, and say to the people there, 'The Kingdom of God has come near you.' But whenever you go into a town and are not welcomed, go out in the streets and say, 'Even the dust from your town that sticks to our feet we wipe off against you. But remember that the Kingdom of God has come near you!' I assure you that on the Judgment Day God will show more mercy to Sodom than to that town!

"How terrible it will be for you, Chorazin! How terrible for you too, Bethsaida! If the miracles which were performed in you had been performed in Tyre and Sidon, the people there would have long ago sat down, put on sackcloth, and sprinkled ashes on themselves, to show that they had turned from their sins! God will show more mercy on the Judgment Day to Tyre and

Sidon than to you. And as for you, Capernaum! Did you want to lift yourself up to heaven? You will be thrown down to hell!"

Jesus said to his disciples, "Whoever listens to you listens to me; whoever rejects you rejects me; and whoever rejects me rejects the one who sent me."

The seventy-two men came back in great joy. "Lord," they said, "even the demons obeyed us when we gave them a command in your name!"

Jesus answered them, "I saw Satan fall like lightning from heaven. Listen! I have given you authority, so that you can walk on snakes and scorpions and overcome all the power of the Enemy, and nothing will hurt you. But don't be glad because the evil spirits obey you; rather be glad because your names are written in heaven."

At that time Jesus was filled with joy by the Holy Spirit and said, "Father, Lord of heaven and earth! I thank you because you have shown to the unlearned what you have hidden from the wise and learned. Yes, Father, this was how you were pleased to have it happen.

"My Father has given me all things. No one knows who the Son is except the Father, and no one knows who the Father is except the Son and those to whom the Son chooses to reveal him."

Then Jesus turned to the disciples and said to them privately, "How fortunate you are to see the things you see! I tell you that many prophets and kings wanted to see what you see, but they could not, and to hear what you hear, but they did not."

A teacher of the Law came up and tried to trap Jesus. "Teacher," he asked, "what must I do to receive eternal life?"

Jesus answered him, "What do the Scriptures say? How do you interpret them?"

The man answered, "'Love the Lord your God with all your heart, with all your soul, with all your strength, and with all your mind'; and 'Love your neighbor as you love yourself.'"

"You are right," Jesus replied; "do this and you will live."

But the teacher of the Law wanted to justify himself, so he asked Jesus, "Who is my neighbor?"

Jesus answered, "There was once a man who was going down from Jerusalem to Jericho when robbers attacked him, stripped him, and beat him up, leaving him half dead. It so happened that a priest was going down that road; but when he saw the man, he walked on by on the other side. In the same way a Levite also came there, went over and looked at the man, and then walked on by on the other side. But a Samaritan who was traveling that way came upon the man, and when he saw him, his heart was filled with pity. He went over to him, poured oil and wine on his wounds and bandaged them; then he put the man on his own animal and took him to an inn, where he took care of him. The next day he took out two silver coins and gave them to the innkeeper. 'Take care of him,' he told the innkeeper, 'and when I come back this way, I will pay you whatever else you spend on him.'"

And Jesus concluded, "In your opinion, which one of these three acted like a neighbor toward the man attacked by the robbers?"

The teacher of the Law answered, "The one who was kind to him."

Jesus replied, "You go, then, and do the same."

As Jesus and his disciples went on their way, he came to a village where a woman named Martha welcomed him in her home. She had a sister named Mary, who sat down at the feet of the Lord and listened to his teaching. Martha was upset over all the work she had to do, so she came and said, "Lord, don't you care that my sister has left me to do all the work by myself? Tell her to come and help me!"

The Lord answered her, "Martha, Martha! You are worried and troubled over so many things, but just one is needed. Mary has chosen the right thing, and it will not be taken away from her." (Luke 10:1–42)

When Jesus finished speaking, a Pharisee invited him to eat with him; so he went in and sat down to eat. The Pharisee was surprised when he noticed that Jesus had not washed before eating. So the Lord said to him, "Now then, you

Pharisees clean the outside of your cup and plate, but inside you are full of violence and evil. Fools! Did not God, who made the outside, also make the inside? But give what is in your cups and plates to the poor, and everything will be ritually clean for you.

"How terrible for you Pharisees! You give to God one tenth of the seasoning herbs, such as mint and rue and all the other herbs, but you neglect justice and love for God. These you should practice, without neglecting the others.

"How terrible for you Pharisees! You love the reserved seats in the synagogues and to be greeted with respect in the marketplaces. How terrible for you! You are like unmarked graves which people walk on without knowing it."

One of the teachers of the Law said to him, "Teacher, when you say this, you insult us too!"

Jesus answered, "How terrible also for you teachers of the Law! You put onto people's backs loads which are hard to carry, but you yourselves will not stretch out a finger to help them carry those loads. How terrible for you! You make fine tombs for the prophets—the very prophets your ancestors murdered. You yourselves admit, then, that you approve of what your ancestors did; they murdered the prophets, and you build their tombs. For this reason the Wisdom of God said, 'I will send them prophets and messengers; they will kill some of them and persecute others.' So the people of this time will be punished for the murder of all the prophets killed since the creation of the world, from the murder of Abel to the murder of Zechariah, who was killed between the altar and the Holy Place. Yes, I tell you, the people of this time will be punished for them all!

"How terrible for you teachers of the Law! You have kept the key that opens the door to the house of knowledge; you yourselves will not go in, and you stop those who are trying to go in!"

When Jesus left that place, the teachers of the Law and the Pharisees began to criticize him bitterly and ask him questions about many things, trying to lay traps for him and catch him saying something wrong. (Luke 11:37–54)

A man in the crowd said to Jesus, "Teacher, tell my brother to divide with me the property our father left us."

Jesus answered him, "Friend, who gave me the right to judge or to divide the property between you two?" And he went on to say to them all, "Watch out and guard yourselves from every kind of greed; because your true life is not made up of the things you own, no matter how rich you may be."

Then Jesus told them this parable: "There was once a rich man who had land which bore good crops. He began to think to himself, 'I don't have a place to keep all my crops. What can I do? This is what I will do,' he told himself; 'I will tear down my barns and build bigger ones, where I will store the grain and all my other goods. Then I will say to myself, Lucky man! You have all the good things you need for many years. Take life easy, eat, drink, and enjoy yourself!' But God said to him, 'You fool! This very night you will have to give up your life; then who will get all these things you have kept for yourself?'"

And Jesus concluded, "This is how it is with those who pile up riches for themselves but are not rich in God's sight." (Luke 12:13–21)

At that time some people were there who told Jesus about the Galileans whom Pilate had killed while they were offering sacrifices to God. Jesus answered them, "Because those Galileans were killed in that way, do you think it proves that they were worse sinners than all other Galileans? No indeed! And I tell you that if you do not turn from your sins, you will all die as they did. What about those eighteen people in Siloam who were killed when the tower fell on them? Do you suppose this proves that they were worse than all the other people living in Jerusalem? No indeed! And I tell you that if you do not turn from your sins, you will all die as they did."

Then Jesus told them this parable: "There was once a man who had a fig tree growing in his vineyard. He went looking for figs on it but found none. So he said to his gardener, 'Look, for three years I have been coming here looking for figs on this fig tree, and I haven't found any. Cut it down! Why should it go on using up the soil?' But the gardener answered, 'Leave it alone, sir, just one more year; I will dig around it and put in some fertilizer. Then if the tree bears figs next year, so much the better; if not, then you can have it cut down.'"

One Sabbath Jesus was teaching in a synagogue. A woman there had an evil spirit that had kept her sick for eighteen years; she was bent over and could not straighten up at all. When Jesus saw her, he called out to her, "Woman, you are free from your sickness!" He placed his hands on her, and at once she straightened herself up and praised God.

The official of the synagogue was angry that Jesus had healed on the Sabbath, so he spoke up and said to the people, "There are six days in which we should work; so come during those days and be healed, but not on the Sabbath!"

The Lord answered him, "You hypocrites! Any one of you would untie your ox or your donkey from the stall and take it out to give it water on the Sabbath. Now here is this descendant of Abraham whom Satan has kept in bonds for eighteen years; should she not be released on the Sabbath?" His answer made his enemies ashamed of themselves, while the people rejoiced over all the wonderful things that he did. (Luke 13:1–17)

As Jesus was walking along, he saw a man who had been born blind. His disciples asked him, "Teacher, whose sin caused him to be born blind? Was it his own or his parents' sin?"

Jesus answered, "His blindness has nothing to do with his sins or his parents' sins. He is blind so that God's power might be seen at work in him. As long as it is day, we must do the work of him who sent me; night is coming when no one can work. While I am in the world, I am the light for the world."

After he said this, Jesus spat on the ground and made some mud with the spittle; he rubbed the mud on the man's eyes and told him, "Go and wash your face in the Pool of Siloam." (This name means "Sent.") So the man went, washed his face, and came back seeing.

His neighbors, then, and the people who had seen him begging before this, asked, "Isn't this the man who used to sit and beg?"

Some said, "He is the one," but others said, "No he isn't; he just looks like him."

So the man himself said, "I am the man."

"How is it that you can now see?" they asked him.

He answered, "The man called Jesus made some mud, rubbed it on my eyes, and told me to go to Siloam and wash my face. So I went, and as soon as I washed, I could see."

"Where is he?" they asked.

"I don't know," he answered.

Then they took to the Pharisees the man who had been blind. The day that Jesus made the mud and cured him of his blindness was a Sabbath. The Pharisees, then, asked the man again how he had received his sight. He told them, "He put some mud on my eyes; I washed my face, and now I can see."

Some of the Pharisees said, "The man who did this cannot be from God, for he does not obey the Sabbath law."

Others, however, said, "How could a man who is a sinner perform such miracles as these?" And there was a division among them.

So the Pharisees asked the man once more, "You say he cured you of your blindness—well, what do you say about him?"

"He is a prophet," the man answered.

The Jewish authorities, however, were not willing to believe that he had been blind and could now see, until they called his parents and asked them, "Is this your son? You say that he was born blind; how is it, then, that he can now see?"

His parents answered, "We know that he is our son, and we know that he was born blind. But we do not know how it is that he is now able to see, nor do we know who cured him of his blindness. Ask him; he is old enough, and he can answer for himself!" His parents said this because they were afraid of the Jewish authorities, who had already agreed that anyone who said he believed that Jesus was the Messiah would be expelled from the synagogue. That is why his parents said, "He is old enough; ask him!"

A second time they called back the man who had been born blind, and said to him, "Promise before God that you will tell the truth! We know that this man who cured you is a sinner."

"I do not know if he is a sinner or not," the man replied. "One thing I do know: I was blind, and now I see."

"What did he do to you?" they asked. "How did he cure you of your blindness?"

"I have already told you," he answered, "and you would not listen. Why do you want to hear it again? Maybe you, too, would like to be his disciples?"

They insulted him and said, "You are that fellow's disciple; but we are Moses' disciples. We know that God spoke to Moses; as for that fellow, however, we do not even know where he comes from!"

The man answered, "What a strange thing that is! You do not know where he comes from, but he cured me of my blindness! We know that God does not listen to sinners; he does listen to people who respect him and do what he wants them to do. Since the beginning of the world nobody has ever heard of anyone giving sight to a person born blind. Unless this man came from God, he would not be able to do a thing."

They answered, "You were born and brought up in sin—and you are trying to teach us?" And they expelled him from the synagogue.

When Jesus heard what had happened, he found the man and asked him, "Do you believe in the Son of Man?"

The man answered, "Tell me who he is, sir, so that I can believe in him!"

Jesus said to him, "You have already seen him, and he is the one who is talking with you now."

"I believe, Lord!" the man said, and knelt down before Jesus.

Jesus said, "I came to this world to judge, so that the blind should see and those who see should become blind."

Some Pharisees who were there with him heard him say this and asked him, "Surely you don't mean that we are blind, too?"

Jesus answered, "If you were blind, then you would not be guilty; but since you claim that you can see, this means that you are still guilty." (John 9:1–41)

Jesus said, "I am telling you the truth: the man who does not enter the sheep pen by the gate, but climbs in some other way, is a thief and a robber. The man who goes in through the gate is the shepherd of the sheep. The gatekeeper opens the gate for him; the sheep hear his voice as he calls his own sheep by name, and he leads them out. When he has brought them out, he goes ahead of them, and the sheep follow him, because they know his voice. They will not follow someone else; instead, they will run away from such a person, because they do not know his voice."

Jesus told them this parable, but they did not understand what he meant.

So Jesus said again, "I am telling you the truth: I am the gate for the sheep. All others who came before me are thieves and robbers, but the sheep did not listen to them. I am the gate. Those who come in by me will be saved; they will come in and go out and find pasture. The thief comes only in order to steal, kill, and destroy. I have come in order that you might have life—life in all its fullness.

"I am the good shepherd, who is willing to die for the sheep. When the hired man, who is not a shepherd and does not own the sheep, sees a wolf coming, he leaves the sheep and runs away; so the wolf snatches the sheep and scatters them. The hired man runs away because he is only a hired man and does not care about the sheep. I am the good shepherd. As the Father knows me and I know the Father, in the same way I know my sheep and they know me. And I am willing to die for them. There are other sheep which belong to me that are not in this sheep pen. I must bring them, too; they will listen to my voice, and they will become one flock with one shepherd.

"The Father loves me because I am willing to give up my life, in order that I may receive it back again. No one takes my life away from me. I give it up of my own free will. I have the right to give it up, and I have the right to take it back. This is what my Father has commanded me to do."

Again there was a division among the people because of these words. Many of them were saying, "He has a demon! He is crazy! Why do you listen to him?"

But others were saying, "A man with a demon could not talk like this! How could a demon give sight to blind people?"

It was winter, and the Festival of the Dedication of the Temple was being celebrated in Jerusalem. Jesus was walking in Solomon's Porch in the Temple, when the people gathered around him and asked, "How long are you going to keep us in suspense? Tell us the plain truth: are you the Messiah?"

Jesus answered, "I have already told you, but you would not believe me. The deeds I do by my Father's authority speak on my behalf; but you will not believe, for you are not my sheep. My sheep listen to my voice; I know them, and they follow me. I give them eternal life, and they shall never die. No one can snatch them away from me. What my Father has given me is greater than everything, and no one can snatch them away from the Father's care. The Father and I are one."

Then the people again picked up stones to throw at him. Jesus said to them, "I have done many good deeds in your presence which the Father gave me to do; for which one of these do you want to stone me?"

They answered, "We do not want to stone you because of any good deeds, but because of your blasphemy! You are only a man, but you are trying to make yourself God!"

Jesus answered, "It is written in your own Law that God said, 'You are gods.' We know that what the scripture says is true forever; and God called those people gods, the people to whom his message was given. As for me, the Father chose me and sent me into the world. How, then, can you say that I blaspheme because I said that I am the Son of God? Do not believe me, then, if I am not doing the things my Father wants me to do. But if I do them, even though you do not believe me, you should at least believe my deeds, in order that you may know once and for all that the Father is in me and that I am in the Father."

Once more they tried to seize Jesus, but he slipped out of their hands.

Jesus then went back again across the Jordan River to the place where John had been baptizing, and he stayed there. Many people came to him. "John performed no miracles," they said, "but everything he said about this man was true." And many people there believed in him. (John 10:1–42)

# Reflections and Questions

## About the Reading

Jesus emphasizes sending his disciples out as sheep among wolves. He says that whoever listens to them is listening to him and to the one who sent him, who is the Father. He reveals these things to the simple people; the wise and knowledgeable are more concerned with their own arguments than with knowing Jesus.

The question arises about what we must do to receive eternal life, and Jesus' answer ends with an instruction to act with kindness. We will be judged according to how we treat our neighbor.

With his parables and miracles, Jesus teaches us who he is. He is the Lord who has authority over religious laws like those of the Sabbath that were very sacred to the Jews.

Jesus is the gate to the sheep pen (meaning heaven). He is the Good Shepherd who takes care of his sheep (meaning humankind).

## Let's Meditate

God has a mission for each of us.

- It is important that you have a personal relationship with Jesus. Who is he to you at this point in your life?

- Jesus calls you to go like a sheep in the midst of wolves. How do you apply this in your circumstances?

- Do you worry about having eternal life? How do you respond to God's call to be merciful to everyone, especially those who suffer?

- What applications do you draw from these parables for your life now? Which of them speaks most to you?

- What part most attracted your attention in the episode of the man who was born blind?

- Do you see yourself as one of the sheep cared for by Jesus, the Good Shepherd? Consider expressing this in a prayer from your heart.

**Ask God**

Take some time for quiet reflection. In your own words, ask God to show you, through this Gospel reading, a clear path to the calling he has revealed to you.

**Think about the Main Idea**

Look for the phrase in the reading that most catches your attention, and repeat it to yourself several times. You might also write it in a journal so that you can revisit it and think about it again.

**Create an Action Plan**

Reading the Bible and praying with it can move us to change.

- How can this reading help you understand your calling better?
- What concrete action can you take to bring your prayer and meditation into daily life?

**Discussion Questions**

1. When an authority of the law asks Jesus, "Who is my neighbor?" Jesus tells the story of a severely beaten man who was rescued by a Samaritan. Keeping in mind the huge cultural and religious division between the Jews and Samaritans in the first century, how would Jesus want you to act toward those with whom you disagree?

2. In the story where Jesus visits his friends Mary and Martha, what about Mary's choice made it better than Martha's? How can you similarly choose "the right thing" in the future?

3. Jesus says that he has come so we may have "life in all its fullness." Based on what you have read or know about Jesus, what would make the life Jesus offers better than other lifestyles?

# 13

# Raising the Dead

Jesus went through towns and villages, teaching the people and making his way toward Jerusalem. Someone asked him, "Sir, will just a few people be saved?"

Jesus answered them, "Do your best to go in through the narrow door; because many people will surely try to go in but will not be able. The master of the house will get up and close the door; then when you stand outside and begin to knock on the door and say, 'Open the door for us, sir!' he will answer you, 'I don't know where you come from!' Then you will answer, 'We ate and drank with you; you taught in our town!' But he will say again, 'I don't know where you come from. Get away from me, all you wicked people!' How you will cry and gnash your teeth when you see Abraham, Isaac, and Jacob, and all the prophets in the Kingdom of God, while you are thrown out! People will come from the east and the west, from the north and the south, and sit down at the feast in the Kingdom of God. Then those who are now last will be first, and those who are now first will be last".

At that same time some Pharisees came to Jesus and said to him, "You must get out of here and go somewhere else, because Herod wants to kill you."

Jesus answered them, "Go and tell that fox: 'I am driving out demons and performing cures today and tomorrow, and on the third day I shall finish my work.' Yet I must be on my way today, tomorrow, and the next day; it is not right for a prophet to be killed anywhere except in Jerusalem.

"Jerusalem, Jerusalem! You kill the prophets, you stone the messengers God has sent you! How many times I wanted to put my arms around all your people, just as a hen gathers her chicks under her wings, but you would not let me! And so your Temple will be abandoned. I assure you that you will not see me until the time comes when you say, 'God bless him who comes in the name of the Lord.'" (Luke 13:22–35)

One Sabbath Jesus went to eat a meal at the home of one of the leading Pharisees; and people were watching Jesus closely. A man whose legs and arms were swollen came to Jesus, and Jesus spoke up and asked the teachers of the Law and the Pharisees, "Does our Law allow healing on the Sabbath or not?"

But they would not say a thing. Jesus took the man, healed him, and sent him away. Then he said to them, "If any one of you had a child or an ox that happened to fall in a well on a Sabbath, would you not pull it out at once on the Sabbath itself?"

But they were not able to answer him about this.

Jesus noticed how some of the guests were choosing the best places, so he told this parable to all of them: "When someone invites you to a wedding feast, do not sit down in the best place. It could happen that someone more important than you has been invited, and your host, who invited both of you, would have to come and say to you, 'Let him have this place.' Then you would be embarrassed and have to sit in the lowest place. Instead, when you are invited, go and sit in the lowest place, so that your host will come to you and say, 'Come on up, my friend, to a better place.' This will bring you honor in the presence of all the other guests. For those who make themselves great will be humbled, and those who humble themselves will be made great."

Then Jesus said to his host, "When you give a lunch or a dinner, do not invite your friends or your brothers or your relatives or your rich neighbors—for they will invite you back, and in this way you will be paid for what you did. When you give a feast, invite the poor, the crippled, the lame, and the blind; and you will be blessed, because they are not able to pay you back. God will repay you on the day the good people rise from death."

When one of the guests sitting at the table heard this, he said to Jesus, "How happy are those who will sit down at the feast in the Kingdom of God!"

Jesus said to him, "There was once a man who was giving a great feast to which he invited many people. When it was time for the feast, he sent his servant to tell his guests, 'Come, everything is ready!' But they all began, one after another, to make excuses. The first one told the servant, 'I have bought a field and must go and look at it; please accept my apologies.' Another one said, 'I have bought five pairs of oxen and am on my way to try them out; please accept my apologies.' Another one said, 'I have just gotten married, and for that reason I cannot come.' The servant went back and told all this to his master. The master was furious and said to his servant, 'Hurry out to the streets and alleys of the town, and bring back the poor, the crippled, the blind, and the lame.' Soon the servant said, 'Your order has been carried out, sir, but there is room for more.' So the master said to the servant, 'Go out to the country roads and lanes and make people come in, so that my house will be full. I tell you all that none of those who were invited will taste my dinner!'"

Once when large crowds of people were going along with Jesus, he turned and said to them, "Those who come to me cannot be my disciples unless they love me more than they love father and mother, wife and children, brothers and sisters, and themselves as well. Those who do not carry their own cross and come after me cannot be my disciples. If one of you is planning to build a tower, you sit down first and figure out what it will cost, to see if you have enough money to finish the job. If you don't, you will not be able to finish the tower after laying the foundation; and all who see what happened will make fun of you. 'You began to build but can't finish the job!' they will say. If a king goes out with ten thousand men to fight another king who comes against him with twenty thousand men, he will sit down first and decide if he is strong enough to face that other king. If he isn't, he will send messengers to meet the other king to ask for terms of peace while he is still a long way off.

In the same way," concluded Jesus, "none of you can be my disciple unless you give up everything you have.

"Salt is good, but if it loses its saltiness, there is no way to make it salty again. It is no good for the soil or for the manure pile; it is thrown away. Listen, then, if you have ears!" (Luke 14:1–35)

One day when many tax collectors and other outcasts came to listen to Jesus, the Pharisees and the teachers of the Law started grumbling, "This man welcomes outcasts and even eats with them!" So Jesus told them this parable:

"Suppose one of you has a hundred sheep and loses one of them—what do you do? You leave the other ninety-nine sheep in the pasture and go looking for the one that got lost until you find it. When you find it, you are so happy that you put it on your shoulders and carry it back home. Then you call your friends and neighbors together and say to them, 'I am so happy I found my lost sheep. Let us celebrate!' In the same way, I tell you, there will be more joy in heaven over one sinner who repents than over ninety-nine respectable people who do not need to repent.

"Or suppose a woman who has ten silver coins loses one of them—what does she do? She lights a lamp, sweeps her house, and looks carefully everywhere until she finds it. When she finds it, she calls her friends and neighbors together, and says to them, 'I am so happy I found the coin I lost. Let us celebrate!' In the same way, I tell you, the angels of God rejoice over one sinner who repents."

Jesus went on to say, "There was once a man who had two sons. The younger one said to him, "Father, give me my share of the property now." So the man divided his property between his two sons. After a few days the younger son sold his part of the property and left home with the money. He went to a country far away, where he wasted his money in reckless living. He spent everything he had. Then a severe famine spread over that country, and he was left without a thing. So he went to work for one of the citizens of that country, who sent him out to his farm to take care of the pigs. He wished he could fill himself with the bean pods the pigs ate, but no one gave him anything to eat. At last he came to his senses and said, "All my father's hired workers have more than they can eat, and here I am about to starve! I will get up and go to my father and say, 'Father, I have sinned against God and against you. I am no longer fit to be called your son; treat me as one of your hired workers.'" So he got up and started back to his father.

"He was still a long way from home when his father saw him; his heart was filled with pity, and he ran, threw his arms around his son, and kissed him. 'Father,' the son said, 'I have sinned against God and against you. I am no longer fit to be called your son.' But the father called to his servants. 'Hurry!' he said. 'Bring the best robe and put it on him. Put a ring on his finger and shoes on his feet. Then go and get the prize calf and kill it, and let us celebrate with a feast! For this son of mine was dead, but now he is alive; he was lost, but now he has been found.' And so the feasting began.

"In the meantime the older son was out in the field. On his way back, when he came close to the house, he heard the music and dancing. So he called one of the servants and asked him, 'What's going on?' 'Your brother has come back home,' the servant answered, 'and your father has killed the prize calf, because he got him back safe and sound.' The older brother was so angry that he would not go into the house; so his father came out and begged him to come in. But he spoke back to his father, 'Look, all these years I have worked for you like a slave, and I have never disobeyed your orders. What have you given me? Not even a goat for me to have a feast with my friends! But this son of yours wasted all your property on prostitutes, and when he comes back home, you kill the prize calf for him!' 'My son,' the father answered, 'you are always here with me, and everything I have is yours. But we had to celebrate and be happy, because your brother was dead, but now he is alive; he was lost, but now he has been found.'" (Luke 15:1–32)

Jesus said to his disciples, "There was once a rich man who had a servant who managed his property. The rich man was told that the manager was wasting his master's money, so he called him in and said, 'What is this I hear about you? Turn in a complete account of your handling of my property, because you cannot be my manager any longer.' The servant said to himself, 'My master is going to dismiss me from my job. What shall I do? I am not strong enough to dig ditches, and I am ashamed to beg. Now I know what I will do! Then when my job is gone, I shall have friends who will welcome me in their homes.' So he called in all the people who were in debt to his master. He asked the first one, 'How much do you owe my master?' 'One hundred barrels of olive oil,' he answered. 'Here is your account,' the manager told him; 'sit down and write fifty.' Then he asked another one, 'And you—how much do you owe?' 'A thousand bushels of wheat,' he answered. 'Here is your account,' the manager told him; 'write eight hundred.' As a result the master of this dishonest manager praised him for doing such a shrewd thing; because the people of this world are much more shrewd in handling their affairs than the people who belong to the light."

And Jesus went on to say, "And so I tell you: make friends for yourselves with worldly wealth, so that when it gives out, you will be welcomed in the eternal home. Whoever is faithful in small matters will be faithful in large ones; whoever is dishonest in small matters will be dishonest in large ones. If, then, you have not been faithful in handling worldly wealth, how can you be trusted with true wealth? And if you have not been faithful with what belongs to someone else, who will give you what belongs to you?

"No servant can be the slave of two masters; such a slave will hate one and love the other or will be loyal to one and despise the other. You cannot serve both God and money."

When the Pharisees heard all this, they made fun of Jesus, because they loved money. Jesus said to them, "You are the ones who make yourselves look right in other people's sight, but God knows your hearts. For the things that are considered of great value by people are worth nothing in God's sight. (Luke 16:1–15)

"There was once a rich man who dressed in the most expensive clothes and lived in great luxury every day. There was also a poor man named Lazarus, covered with sores, who used to be brought to the rich man's door, hoping to eat the bits of food that fell from the rich man's table. Even the dogs would come and lick his sores. The poor man died and was carried by the angels to sit beside Abraham at the feast in heaven. The rich man died and was buried, and in Hades, where he was in great pain, he looked up and saw Abraham, far away, with Lazarus at his side. So he called out, 'Father Abraham! Take pity on me, and send Lazarus to dip his finger in some water and cool off my tongue, because I am in great pain in this fire!' But Abraham said, 'Remember, my son, that in your lifetime you were given all the good things, while Lazarus got all the bad things. But now he is enjoying himself here, while you are in pain. Besides all that, there is a deep pit lying between us, so that those who want to cross over from here to you cannot do so, nor can anyone cross over to us from where you are.' The rich man said, 'Then I beg you, father Abraham, send Lazarus to my father's house, where I have five brothers. Let him go and warn them so that they, at least, will not come to this place of pain.' Abraham said, 'Your brothers have Moses and the prophets to warn them; your brothers should listen to what they say.' The rich man answered, 'That is not enough, father Abraham! But if someone were to rise from death and go to them, then they would turn from their sins.' But Abraham said, 'If they will not listen to Moses and the prophets, they will not be convinced even if someone were to rise from death.'" (Luke 16:19–31)

Jesus said to his disciples, "Things that make people fall into sin are bound to happen, but how terrible for the one who makes them happen! It would be better for him if a large millstone were tied around his neck and he were thrown into the sea than for him to cause one of these little ones to sin. So watch what you do!

"If your brother sins, rebuke him, and if he repents, forgive him. If he sins against you seven times in one day, and each time he comes to you saying, 'I repent,' you must forgive him."

The apostles said to the Lord, "Make our faith greater."

The Lord answered, "If you had faith as big as a mustard seed, you could say to this mulberry tree, 'Pull yourself up by the roots and plant yourself in the sea!' and it would obey you.

"Suppose one of you has a servant who is plowing or looking after the sheep. When he comes in from the field, do you tell him to hurry along and eat his meal? Of course not! Instead, you say to him, 'Get my supper ready, then put on your apron and wait on me while I eat and drink; after that you may have your meal.' The servant does not deserve thanks for obeying orders, does he? It is the same with you; when you have done all you have been told to do, say, 'We are ordinary servants; we have only done our duty.'" (Luke 17:1–10)

A man named Lazarus, who lived in Bethany, became sick. Bethany was the town where Mary and her sister Martha lived. (This Mary was the one who poured the perfume on the Lord's feet and wiped them with her hair; it was her brother Lazarus who was sick.) The sisters sent Jesus a message: "Lord, your dear friend is sick."

When Jesus heard it, he said, "The final result of this sickness will not be the death of Lazarus; this has happened in order to bring glory to God, and it will be the means by which the Son of God will receive glory."

Jesus loved Martha and her sister and Lazarus. Yet when he received the news that Lazarus was sick, he stayed where he was for two more days. Then he said to the disciples, "Let us go back to Judea."

"Teacher," the disciples answered, "just a short time ago the people there wanted to stone you; and are you planning to go back?"

Jesus said, "A day has twelve hours, doesn't it? So those who walk in broad daylight do not stumble, for they see the light of this world. But if they walk during the night they stumble, because they have no light." Jesus said this and then added, "Our friend Lazarus has fallen asleep, but I will go and wake him up."

The disciples answered, "If he is asleep, Lord, he will get well."

Jesus meant that Lazarus had died, but they thought he meant natural sleep. So Jesus told them plainly, "Lazarus is dead, but for your sake I am glad that I was not with him, so that you will believe. Let us go to him."

Thomas (called the Twin) said to his fellow disciples, "Let us all go along with the Teacher, so that we may die with him!"

When Jesus arrived, he found that Lazarus had been buried four days before. Bethany was less than two miles from Jerusalem, and many Judeans had come to see Martha and Mary to comfort them about their brother's death.

When Martha heard that Jesus was coming, she went out to meet him, but Mary stayed in the house. Martha said to Jesus, "If you had been here, Lord, my brother would not have died! But I know that even now God will give you whatever you ask him for."

"Your brother will rise to life," Jesus told her.

"I know," she replied, "that he will rise to life on the last day."

Jesus said to her, "I am the resurrection and the life. Those who believe in me will live, even though they die; and those who live and believe in me will never die. Do you believe this?"

"Yes, Lord!" she answered. "I do believe that you are the Messiah, the Son of God, who was to come into the world."

After Martha said this, she went back and called her sister Mary privately. "The Teacher is here," she told her, "and is asking for you." When Mary heard this, she got up and hurried out to meet him. (Jesus had not yet arrived in the village, but was still in the place where Martha had met him.) The people who were in the house with Mary comforting her followed her when they saw her get up and hurry out. They thought that she was going to the grave to weep there.

Mary arrived where Jesus was, and as soon as she saw him, she fell at his feet. "Lord," she said, "if you had been here, my brother would not have died!"

Jesus saw her weeping, and he saw how the people with her were weeping also; his heart was touched, and he was deeply moved. "Where have you buried him?" he asked them.

"Come and see, Lord," they answered.

Jesus wept. "See how much he loved him!" the people said.

But some of them said, "He gave sight to the blind man, didn't he? Could he not have kept Lazarus from dying?

Deeply moved once more, Jesus went to the tomb, which was a cave with a stone placed at the entrance. "Take the stone away!" Jesus ordered.

Martha, the dead man's sister, answered, "There will be a bad smell, Lord. He has been buried four days!"

Jesus said to her, "Didn't I tell you that you would see God's glory if you believed?" They took the stone away. Jesus looked up and said, "I thank you, Father, that you listen to me. I know that you always listen to me, but I say this for the sake of the people here, so that they will believe that you sent me." After he had said this, he called out in a loud voice, "Lazarus, come out!" He came out, his hands and feet wrapped in grave cloths, and with a cloth around his face. "Untie him," Jesus told them, "and let him go."

Many of the people who had come to visit Mary saw what Jesus did, and they believed in him. But some of them returned to the Pharisees and told them what Jesus had done. So the Pharisees and the chief priests met with the Council and said, "What shall we do? Look at all the miracles this man is performing! If we let him go on in this way, everyone will believe in him, and the Roman authorities will take action and destroy our Temple and our nation!"

One of them, named Caiaphas, who was High Priest that year, said, "What fools you are! Don't you realize that it is better for you to have one man die for the people, instead of having the whole nation destroyed?" Actually, he did not say this of his own accord; rather, as he was High Priest that year, he was prophesying that Jesus was going to die for the Jewish people, and not only for them, but also to bring together into one body all the scattered people of God.

From that day on the Jewish authorities made plans to kill Jesus. So Jesus did not travel openly in Judea, but left and went to a place near the desert, to a town named Ephraim, where he stayed with the disciples. (John 11:1–54)

# Reflections and Questions

## About the Reading

Carefully consider the story of the feast in this chapter. Jesus is the one who invites us, but many people make excuses. His feast is open to everyone, but to partake you have to love Jesus more than everything else.

We read a touching story of the son who wasted his inheritance. His father was waiting for him and received him back with affection and without questioning him. Compare that to the attitude of the other son who did not accept the father's mercy.

The distance that separates the poor man and the rich man, who both died, is remarkable. It offers a new perspective on everything that happened with Lazarus, the friend of Jesus who died. His sisters had sent messages for Jesus to come, but Jesus was late and Lazarus was dead when he arrived. However, Jesus is the "resurrection and the life." He thanked God, saying: "I know that you always listen to me." Then he ordered Lazarus to "come out."

## Let's Meditate

God has a mission for each of us.

- Through these readings, Jesus extends to us an invitation to his kingdom. Do you desire to accept that invitation? Considering the excuses given in this reading, which ones might appeal to you, and why?

- If you compare the parable of the merciful father to your life, which of the two sons describes you better? Are you able to feel God's unconditional love toward you?

- Mary complained because Jesus was not there when her brother died, after she called for him to come. Do you also get angry with Jesus when he doesn't do what you ask him to do?

- Can you pray with confidence, "Father, I thank you because you always listen to me"?

- When you are in a very difficult situation, how do you feel when Jesus calls you to come out of it?

## Ask God

Take some time for quiet reflection. In your own words, ask God to show you, through this Gospel reading, a clear path to the calling he has revealed to you.

## Think about the Main Idea

Look for the phrase in the reading that most catches your attention, and repeat it to yourself several times. You might also write it in a journal so that you can revisit it and think about it again.

## Create an Action Plan

Reading the Bible and praying with it can move us to change.

- How can this reading help you understand your calling better?
- What concrete action can you take to bring your prayer and meditation into daily life?

## Discussion Questions

1. Jesus shares a story about a shepherd who leaves his sheep to find the one who is lost. How does it feel to hear that Jesus will do the same to find you when you are lost?

2. Jesus paints a vivid contrast between the attitude of the younger son, who receives a warm welcome from his father that he felt he didn't deserve, and the older son, who feels unappreciated for his years of faithful service. When do you feel more like the younger son? How about the older son?

3. Jesus warns his disciples and the Pharisees, "You cannot serve both God and money." Jesus is referring to our tendency to be more devoted to money, and all that money can buy, than to him. How is money a temptation for you? What or who tends to be your master?

# 14

# Welcomed as King

The time for the Passover Festival was near, and many people went up from the country to Jerusalem to perform the ritual of purification before the festival. They were looking for Jesus, and as they gathered in the Temple, they asked one another, "What do you think? Surely he will not come to the festival, will he?" The chief priests and the Pharisees had given orders that if anyone knew where Jesus was, he must report it, so that they could arrest him. (John 11:55–57)

As Jesus made his way to Jerusalem, he went along the border between Samaria and Galilee. He was going into a village when he was met by ten men suffering from a dreaded skin disease. They stood at a distance and shouted, "Jesus! Master! Have pity on us!"

Jesus saw them and said to them, "Go and let the priests examine you."

On the way they were made clean. When one of them saw that he was healed, he came back, praising God in a loud voice. He threw himself to the ground at Jesus' feet and thanked him. The man was a Samaritan. Jesus spoke up, "There were ten who were healed; where are the other nine? Why is this foreigner the only one who came back to give thanks to God?" And Jesus said to him, "Get up and go; your faith has made you well."

Some Pharisees asked Jesus when the Kingdom of God would come. His answer was, "The Kingdom of God does not come in such a way as to be seen. No one will say, 'Look, here it is!' or, 'There it is!' because the Kingdom of God is within you."

Then he said to the disciples, "The time will come when you will wish you could see one of the days of the Son of Man, but you will not see it. There will be those who will say to you, 'Look, over there!' or, 'Look, over here!' But don't go out looking for it. As the lightning flashes across the sky and lights it up from one side to the other, so will the Son of Man be in his day. But first he must suffer much and be rejected by the people of this day. As it was in the time of Noah so shall it be in the days of the Son of Man. Everybody kept on eating and drinking, and men and women married, up to the very day Noah went into the boat and the flood came and killed them all. It will be as it was in the time of Lot. Everybody kept on eating and drinking, buying and sell-ing, planting and building. On the day Lot left Sodom, fire and sulfur rained down from heaven and killed them all. That is how it will be on the day the Son of Man is revealed.

"On that day someone who is on the roof of a house must not go down into the house to get any belongings; in the same way anyone who is out in the field must not go back to the house. Remember Lot's wife! Those who try to save their own life will lose it; those who lose their life will save it. On that night, I tell you, there will be two people sleeping in the same bed: one will be taken away, the other will be left behind. Two women will be grinding meal together: one will be taken away, the other will be left behind."

The disciples asked him, "Where, Lord?"

Jesus answered, "Wherever there is a dead body, the vultures will gather." (Luke 17:11–37)

Then Jesus told his disciples a parable to teach them that they should always pray and never become discouraged. "In a certain town there was a judge who neither feared God nor respected people. And there was a widow in that same town who kept coming to him and pleading for her rights, saying, 'Help me against my opponent!' For a long time the judge refused to act, but at last he said to himself, 'Even though I don't fear God or respect people, yet because of all the trouble this widow is giving me, I will see to it that she gets her rights. If I don't, she will keep on coming and finally wear me out!'"

And the Lord continued, "Listen to what that corrupt judge said. Now, will God not judge in favor of his own people who cry to him day and night for help? Will he be slow to help them? I tell you, he will judge in their favor and do it quickly. But will the Son of Man find faith on earth when he comes?"

Jesus also told this parable to people who were sure of their own goodness and despised everybody else. "Once there were two men who went up to the Temple to pray: one was a Pharisee, the other a tax collector. The Pharisee stood apart by himself and prayed, 'I thank you, God, that I am not greedy, dishonest, or an adulterer, like everybody else. I thank you that I am not like that tax collector over there. I fast two days a week, and I give you one tenth of all my income.' But the tax collector stood at a distance and would not even raise his face to heaven, but beat on his breast and said, 'God, have pity on me, a sinner!' I tell you," said Jesus, "the tax collector, and not the Pharisee, was in the right with God when he went home. For those who make themselves great will be humbled, and those who humble themselves will be made great." (Luke 18:1–14)

When Jesus finished saying these things, he left Galilee and went to the territory of Judea on the other side of the Jordan River. Large crowds followed him, and he healed them there.

Some Pharisees came to him and tried to trap him by asking, "Does our Law allow a man to divorce his wife for whatever reason he wishes?"

Jesus answered, "Haven't you read the scripture that says that in the beginning the Creator made people male and female? And God said, 'For this reason a man will leave his father and mother and unite with his wife, and the two will become one.' So they are no longer two, but one. No human being must separate, then, what God has joined together."

The Pharisees asked him, "Why, then, did Moses give the law for a man to hand his wife a divorce notice and send her away?"

Jesus answered, "Moses gave you permission to divorce your wives because you are so hard to teach. But it was not like that at the time of creation. I tell you, then, that any man who divorces his wife for any cause other than her unfaithfulness, commits adultery if he marries some other woman."

His disciples said to him, "If this is how it is between a man and his wife, it is better not to marry."

Jesus answered, "This teaching does not apply to everyone, but only to those to whom God has given it. For there are different reasons why men cannot marry: some, because they were born that way; others, because men made them that way; and others do not marry for the sake of the Kingdom of heaven. Let him who can accept this teaching do so." (Matthew 19:1–12)

Some people brought children to Jesus for him to place his hands on them, but the disciples scolded the people. When Jesus noticed this, he was angry and said to his disciples, "Let the children come to me, and do not stop them, because the Kingdom of God belongs to such as these. I assure you that whoever does not receive the Kingdom of God like a child will never enter it." Then he took the children in his arms, placed his hands on each of them, and blessed them.

As Jesus was starting on his way again, a man ran up, knelt before him, and asked him, "Good Teacher, what must I do to receive eternal life?"

"Why do you call me good?" Jesus asked him. "No one is good except God alone. You know the commandments: 'Do not commit murder; do not commit adultery; do not steal; do not accuse anyone falsely; do not cheat; respect your father and your mother.'"

"Teacher," the man said, "ever since I was young, I have obeyed all these commandments."

Jesus looked straight at him with love and said, "You need only one thing. Go and sell all you have and give the money to the poor, and you will have riches in heaven; then come and follow me." When the man heard this, gloom spread over his face, and he went away sad, because he was very rich.

Jesus looked around at his disciples and said to them, "How hard it will be for rich people to enter the Kingdom of God!"

The disciples were shocked at these words, but Jesus went on to say, "My children, how hard it is to enter the Kingdom of God! It is much harder for a rich person to enter the Kingdom of God than for a camel to go through the eye of a needle."

At this the disciples were completely amazed and asked one another, "Who, then, can be saved?"

Jesus looked straight at them and answered, "This is impossible for human beings but not for God; everything is possible for God."

Then Peter spoke up, "Look, we have left everything and followed you."

"Yes," Jesus said to them, "and I tell you that those who leave home or brothers or sisters or mother or father or children or fields for me and for the gospel, will receive much more in this present age. They will receive a hundred times more houses, brothers, sisters, mothers, children, and fields—and persecutions as well; and in the age to come they will receive eternal life." (Mark 10:13–30)

"The Kingdom of heaven is like this. Once there was a man who went out early in the morning to hire some men to work in his vineyard. He agreed to pay them the regular wage, a silver coin a day, and sent them to work in his vineyard. He went out again to the marketplace at nine o'clock and saw some men standing there doing nothing, so he told them, 'You also go and work in the vineyard, and I will pay you a fair wage.' So they went. Then at twelve o'clock and again at three o'clock he did the same thing. It was nearly five o'clock when he went to the marketplace and saw some other men still standing there. 'Why are you wasting the whole day here doing nothing?' he asked them. 'No one hired us,' they answered. 'Well, then, you go and work in the vineyard,' he told them.

"When evening came, the owner told his foreman, 'Call the workers and pay them their wages, starting with those who were hired last and ending with those who were hired first.' The men who had begun to work at five o'clock were paid a silver coin each. So when the men who were the first to be hired came to be paid, they thought they would get more; but they too were given a silver coin each. They took their money and started grumbling against the employer. 'These men who were hired last worked only one hour,' they said, 'while we put up with a whole day's work in the hot sun—yet you paid them the same as you paid us!' 'Listen, friend,' the owner answered one of them, 'I have not cheated you. After all, you agreed to do a day's work for one silver coin. Now take your pay and go home. I want to give this man who was hired last as much as I gave you. Don't I have the right to do as I wish with my own money? Or are you jealous because I am generous?'"

And Jesus concluded, "So those who are last will be first, and those who are first will be last." (Matthew 20:1–16)

Jesus and his disciples were now on the road going up to Jerusalem. Jesus was going ahead of the disciples, who were filled with alarm; the people who followed behind were afraid. Once again Jesus took the twelve disciples aside and spoke of the things that were going to happen to him. "Listen," he told them, "we are going up to Jerusalem where the Son of Man will be handed over to the chief priests and the teachers of the Law. They will condemn him to death and then hand him over to the Gentiles, who will make fun of him, spit on him, whip him, and kill him; but three days later he will rise to life."

Then James and John, the sons of Zebedee, came to Jesus. "Teacher," they said, "there is something we want you to do for us."

"What is it?" Jesus asked them.

They answered, "When you sit on your throne in your glorious Kingdom, we want you to let us sit with you, one at your right and one at your left."

Jesus said to them, "You don't know what you are asking for. Can you drink the cup of suffering that I must drink? Can you be baptized in the way I must be baptized?"

"We can," they answered.

Jesus said to them, "You will indeed drink the cup I must drink and be baptized in the way I must be baptized. But I do not have the right to choose who will sit at my right and my left. It is God who will give these places to those for whom he has prepared them."

When the other ten disciples heard about it, they became angry with James and John. So Jesus called them all together to him and said, "You know that those who are considered rulers of the heathen have power over them, and the leaders have complete authority. This, however, is not the way it is among you. If one of you wants to be great, you must be the servant of the rest; and if one of you wants to be first, you must be the slave of all. For even the Son of Man did not come to be served; he came to serve and to give his life to redeem many people." (Mark 10:32–45)

As Jesus was coming near Jericho, there was a blind man sitting by the road, begging. When he heard the crowd passing by, he asked, "What is this?"

"Jesus of Nazareth is passing by," they told him.

He cried out, "Jesus! Son of David! Have mercy on me!"

The people in front scolded him and told him to be quiet. But he shouted even more loudly, "Son of David! Have mercy on me!"

So Jesus stopped and ordered the blind man to be brought to him. When he came near, Jesus asked him, "What do you want me to do for you?"

"Sir," he answered, "I want to see again."

Jesus said to him, "Then see! Your faith has made you well."

At once he was able to see, and he followed Jesus, giving thanks to God. When the crowd saw it, they all praised God. (Luke 18:35–43)

Jesus went on into Jericho and was passing through. There was a chief tax collector there named Zacchaeus, who was rich. He was trying to see who Jesus was, but he was a little man and could not see Jesus because of the crowd. So he ran ahead of the crowd and climbed a sycamore tree to see Jesus, who was going to pass that way. When Jesus came to that place, he looked up and said to Zacchaeus, "Hurry down, Zacchaeus, because I must stay in your house today."

Zacchaeus hurried down and welcomed him with great joy. All the people who saw it started grumbling, "This man has gone as a guest to the home of a sinner!"

Zacchaeus stood up and said to the Lord, "Listen, sir! I will give half my belongings to the poor, and if I have cheated anyone, I will pay back four times as much."

Jesus said to him, "Salvation has come to this house today, for this man, also, is a descendant of Abraham. The Son of Man came to seek and to save the lost."

While the people were listening to this, Jesus continued and told them a parable. He was now almost at Jerusalem, and they supposed that the Kingdom of God was just about to appear. So he said, "There was once a man of high rank who was going to a country far away to be made king, after which he planned to come back home. Before he left, he called his ten servants and gave them each a gold coin and told them, 'See what you can earn with this while I am gone.' Now, his own people hated him, and so they sent messengers after him to say, 'We don't want this man to be our king.'

"The man was made king and came back. At once he ordered his servants to appear before him, in order to find out how much they had earned. The first one came and said, 'Sir, I have earned ten gold coins with the one you gave me.' 'Well done,' he said; 'you are a good servant! Since you were faithful in small matters, I will put you in charge of ten cities.' The second servant came and said, 'Sir, I have earned five gold coins with the one you gave me.' To this one he said, 'You will be in charge of five cities.' Another servant came and said, 'Sir, here is your gold coin; I kept it hidden in a handkerchief. I was afraid of you, because you are a hard man. You take what is not yours and reap what you did not plant.' He said to him, 'You bad servant! I will use your own words to condemn you! You know that I am a hard man, taking what is not mine and reaping what I have not planted. Well, then, why didn't you put my money in the bank? Then I would have received it back with interest when I returned.' Then he said to those who were standing there, 'Take the gold coin away from him and give it to the servant who has ten coins.' But they said to him, 'Sir, he already has ten coins!' 'I tell you,' he replied, 'that to those who have something, even more will be given; but those who have nothing, even the little that they have will be taken away from them. Now, as for those enemies of mine who did not want me to be their king, bring them here and kill them in my presence!'" (Luke 19:1–27)

As Jesus and his disciples approached Jerusalem, they came to Bethphage at the Mount of Olives. There Jesus sent two of the disciples on ahead with these instructions: "Go to the village there ahead of you, and at once you will find a donkey tied up with her colt beside her. Untie them and bring them to me. And if anyone says anything, tell him, 'The Master needs them'; and then he will let them go at once."

This happened in order to make come true what the prophet had said: "Tell the city of Zion, Look, your king is coming to you! He is humble and rides on a donkey and on a colt, the foal of a donkey."

So the disciples went and did what Jesus had told them to do: they brought the donkey and the colt, threw their cloaks over them, and Jesus got on. A large crowd of people spread their cloaks on the road while others cut branches from the trees and spread them on the road. The crowds walking in front of Jesus and those walking behind began to shout:

"[Hosanna,] praise to David's Son!

"God bless him who comes in the name of the Lord!

"Praise be to God!" (Matthew 21:1–9)

Then some of the Pharisees in the crowd spoke to Jesus. "Teacher," they said, "command your disciples to be quiet!"

Jesus answered, "I tell you that if they keep quiet, the stones themselves will start shouting." (Luke 19:39–40)

His disciples did not understand this at the time; but when Jesus had been raised to glory, they remembered that the scripture said this about him and that they had done this for him.

The people who had been with Jesus when he called Lazarus out of the grave and raised him from death had reported what had happened. That was why the crowd met him—because they heard that he had performed this miracle. The Pharisees then said to one another, "You see, we are not succeeding at all! Look, the whole world is following him!" (John 12:16–19)

# Reflections and Questions

### About the Reading

We see that persistence in prayer is paramount to Jesus. He explains it in many ways—for example, with the widow who constantly petitioned the judge, or the tax collector who was considered a sinner by all but whose prayer was heard because of his humility.

Many question Jesus about the law; then one man asks him how to receive eternal life. He has kept the Jewish law since childhood; however, Jesus invites him to take another step—to let go of his riches and follow him, but the man does not want to follow Jesus that much.

Those who have left everything to follow Jesus have questions about their own futures. Jesus is clear, assuring them that those who leave everything to follow him and to preach the Good News will receive a hundred times more, even in the midst of persecution.

### Let's Meditate

God has a mission for each of us.

- The Lord instructs us to pray always without getting discouraged. What is your relationship with God through prayer? Do you pray frequently? How does—or can—your prayer life encourage others?

- A man who has obeyed everything in the Jewish law since his youth approaches Jesus. He is a good example. If Jesus were to ask you today about obeying the Ten Commandments, could you say that you have always kept them? How can you do better to obey God's law, and why do you think this is important, as Jesus certainly affirmed?

- The rich man goes away sad because he is not ready to follow Jesus. In your encounters with Jesus, do you have joy and peace because you are able to let go of things and follow him? Or do you feel you don't want to pray because you worry that Jesus will ask you for something you don't want to give up? How do you resolve this situation?

- These words of Jesus are clear for those who have left everything to follow him: "They will receive a hundred times more . . . and persecutions as well; and in the age to come they will receive eternal life." Do you realize that this promise also applies to you? What will you do to fulfill it?

- Jesus invites himself to the house of Zacchaeus, who with great joy gives away half of his property and returns four times more than he stole. Jesus tells him, "Salvation has come to this house today." What is your frame of mind when you meet Jesus? Can Jesus say to you that salvation has come into your life?

## Ask God

Take some time for quiet reflection. In your own words, ask God to show you, through this Gospel reading, a clear path to the calling he has revealed to you.

## Think about the Main Idea

Look for the phrase in the reading that most catches your attention, and repeat it to yourself several times. You might also write it in a journal so that you can revisit it and think about it again.

## Create an Action Plan

Reading the Bible and praying with it can move us to change.

- How can this reading help you understand your calling better?
- What concrete action can you take to bring your prayer and meditation into daily life?

## Discussion Questions

1. When Jesus heals ten men who have a skin disease, only one returns to Jesus to thank him. What is the difference between that man's attitude and the other nine? How do you see traces of your own attitude in that of the one man, as well as the attitudes of the other nine?

2. How is the Pharisee's attitude different from the tax collector's? What does Jesus mean when he says, "Those who make themselves great

will be humbled, and those who humble themselves will be made great"?

3. When Jesus enters Jerusalem on a donkey (a day that is now often remembered as Palm Sunday), the crowd spreads cloaks and palm branches on the road ahead of Jesus. The people shout "Hosanna" as Jesus enters Jerusalem, a Hebrew word meaning "save us." What do you think the people in the first century wanted Jesus to save them from? What would you like Jesus to save you from today?

# 15

# Authority Questioned

He came closer to the city, and when he saw it, he wept over it, saying, "If you only knew today what is needed for peace! But now you cannot see it! The time will come when your enemies will surround you with barricades, blockade you, and close in on you from every side. They will completely destroy you and the people within your walls; not a single stone will they leave in its place, because you did not recognize the time when God came to save you!" (Luke 19:41–44)

Jesus entered Jerusalem, went into the Temple, and looked around at everything. But since it was already late in the day, he went out to Bethany with the twelve disciples.

The next day, as they were coming back from Bethany, Jesus was hungry. He saw in the distance a fig tree covered with leaves, so he went to see if he could find any figs on it. But when he came to it, he found only leaves, because it was not the right time for figs. Jesus said to the fig tree, "No one shall ever eat figs from you again!"

And his disciples heard him.

When they arrived in Jerusalem, Jesus went to the Temple and began to drive out all those who were buying and selling. He overturned the tables of the moneychangers and the stools of those who sold pigeons, and he would not let anyone carry anything through the Temple courtyards. He then taught the people: "It is written in the Scriptures that God said, 'My Temple will be called a house of prayer for the people of all nations.' But you have turned it into a hideout for thieves!"

The chief priests and the teachers of the Law heard of this, so they began looking for some way to kill Jesus. They were afraid of him, because the whole crowd was amazed at his teaching. (Mark 11:11–18)

The Jewish authorities came back at him with a question, "What miracle can you perform to show us that you have the right to do this?"

Jesus answered, "Tear down this Temple, and in three days I will build it again."

"Are you going to build it again in three days?" they asked him. "It has taken forty-six years to build this Temple!"

But the temple Jesus was speaking about was his body. So when he was raised from death, his disciples remembered that he had said this, and they believed the scripture and what Jesus had said. (John 2:18–22)

Some Greeks were among those who had gone to Jerusalem to worship during the festival. They went to Philip (he was from Bethsaida in Galilee) and said, "Sir, we want to see Jesus."

Philip went and told Andrew, and the two of them went and told Jesus. Jesus answered them, "The hour has now come for the Son of Man to receive great glory. I am telling you the truth: a grain of wheat remains no more than a single grain unless it is dropped into the ground and dies. If it does die, then it produces many grains. Those who love their own life will lose it; those who hate their own life in this world will keep it for life eternal. Whoever wants to serve me must follow me, so that my servant will be with me where I am. And my Father will honor anyone who serves me.

"Now my heart is troubled—and what shall I say? Shall I say, 'Father, do not let this hour come upon me'? But that is why I came—so that I might go through this hour of suffering. Father, bring glory to your name!"

Then a voice spoke from heaven, "I have brought glory to it, and I will do so again."

The crowd standing there heard the voice, and some of them said it was thunder, while others said, "An angel spoke to him!"

But Jesus said to them, "It was not for my sake that this voice spoke, but for yours. Now is the time for this world to be judged; now the ruler of this world will be overthrown. When I am lifted up from the earth, I will draw everyone to me." (In saying this he indicated the kind of death he was going to suffer.)

The crowd answered, "Our Law tells us that the Messiah will live forever. How, then, can you say that the Son of Man must be lifted up? Who is this Son of Man?"

Jesus answered, "The light will be among you a little longer. Continue on your way while you have the light, so that the darkness will not come upon you; for the one who walks in the dark does not know where he is going. Believe in the light, then, while you have it, so that you will be the people of the light."

After Jesus said this, he went off and hid himself from them.

Even though he had performed all these miracles in their presence, they did not believe in him, so that what the prophet Isaiah had said might come true: "Lord, who believed the message we told? To whom did the Lord reveal his power?"

And so they were not able to believe, because Isaiah also said, "God has blinded their eyes and closed their minds, so that their eyes would not see, and their minds would not understand, and they would not turn to me, says God, for me to heal them." Isaiah said this because he saw Jesus' glory and spoke about him.

Even then, many Jewish authorities believed in Jesus; but because of the Pharisees they did not talk about it openly, so as not to be expelled from the synagogue. They loved human approval rather than the approval of God.

Jesus said in a loud voice, "Whoever believes in me believes not only in me but also in him who sent me. Whoever sees me sees also him who sent me. I have come into the world as light, so that everyone who believes in me should not remain in the darkness. If people hear my message and do not obey it, I will not judge them. I came, not to judge the world, but to save it. Those who reject me and do not accept my message have one who will judge them. The words I have spoken will be their judge on the last day! This is true, because I have not spoken on my own authority, but the Father who sent me has commanded me what I must say and speak. And I know that his command brings eternal life. What I say, then, is what the Father has told me to say." (John 12:20–50)

When evening came, Jesus and his disciples left the city. Early next morning, as they walked along the road, they saw the fig tree. It was dead all the way down to its roots. Peter remembered what had happened and said to Jesus, "Look, Teacher, the fig tree you cursed has died!"

Jesus answered them, "Have faith in God. I assure you that whoever tells this hill to get up and throw itself in the sea and does not doubt in his heart, but believes that what he says will happen, it will be done for him. For this reason I tell you: When you pray and ask for something, believe that you have received it, and you will be given whatever you ask for. And when you stand and pray, forgive anything you may have against anyone, so that your Father in heaven will forgive the wrongs you have done. If you do not forgive others, your Father in heaven will not forgive the wrongs you have done." (Mark 11:19–26)

Jesus came back to the Temple; and as he taught, the chief priests and the elders came to him and asked, "What right do you have to do these things? Who gave you such right?"

Jesus answered them, "I will ask you just one question, and if you give me an answer, I will tell you what right I have to do these things. Where did John's right to baptize come from: was it from God or from human beings?"

They started to argue among themselves, "What shall we say? If we answer, 'From God,' he will say to us, 'Why, then, did you not believe John?' But if we say, 'From human beings,' we are afraid of what the people might do, because they are all convinced that John was a prophet." So they answered Jesus, "We don't know."

And he said to them, "Neither will I tell you, then, by what right I do these things.

"Now, what do you think? There was once a man who had two sons. He went to the older one and said, 'Son, go and work in the vineyard today.' 'I don't want to,' he answered, but later he changed his mind and went. Then the father went to the other son and said the same thing. 'Yes, sir,' he answered, but he did not go. Which one of the two did what his father wanted?"

"The older one," they answered.

So Jesus said to them, "I tell you: the tax collectors and the prostitutes are going into the Kingdom of God ahead of you. For John the Baptist came to you showing you the right path to take, and you would not believe him; but the tax collectors and the prostitutes believed him. Even when you saw this, you did not later change your minds and believe him.

"Listen to another parable," Jesus said. "There was once a landowner who planted a vineyard, put a fence around it, dug a hole for the wine press, and built a watchtower. Then he rented the vineyard to tenants and left home on a trip. When the time came to gather the grapes, he sent his slaves to the tenants to receive his share of the harvest. The tenants grabbed his slaves, beat one, killed another, and stoned another. Again the man sent other slaves, more than the first time, and the tenants treated them the same way. Last of all he sent his son to them. 'Surely they will respect my son,' he said. But when the tenants saw the son, they said to themselves, 'This is the owner's son. Come on, let's kill him, and we will get his property!' So they grabbed him, threw him out of the vineyard, and killed him.

"Now, when the owner of the vineyard comes, what will he do to those tenants?" Jesus asked.

"He will certainly kill those evil men," they answered, "and rent the vineyard out to other tenants, who will give him his share of the harvest at the right time."

Jesus said to them, "Haven't you ever read what the Scriptures say? 'The stone which the builders rejected as worthless turned out to be the most

important of all. This was done by the Lord; what a wonderful sight it is!'
And so I tell you," added Jesus, "the Kingdom of God will be taken away
from you and given to a people who will produce the proper fruits."

The chief priests and the Pharisees heard Jesus' parables and knew that he
was talking about them, so they tried to arrest him. But they were afraid of
the crowds, who considered Jesus to be a prophet. (Matthew 21:23–46)

Jesus again used parables in talking to the people. "The Kingdom of heaven is
like this. Once there was a king who prepared a wedding feast for his son. He
sent his servants to tell the invited guests to come to the feast, but they did
not want to come. So he sent other servants with this message for the guests:
'My feast is ready now; my steers and prize calves have been butchered, and
everything is ready. Come to the wedding feast!' But the invited guests paid
no attention and went about their business: one went to his farm, another to
his store, while others grabbed the servants, beat them, and killed them. The
king was very angry; so he sent his soldiers, who killed those murderers and
burned down their city. Then he called his servants and said to them, 'My
wedding feast is ready, but the people I invited did not deserve it. Now go to
the main streets and invite to the feast as many people as you find.' So the
servants went out into the streets and gathered all the people they could find,
good and bad alike; and the wedding hall was filled with people.

"The king went in to look at the guests and saw a man who was not
wearing wedding clothes. 'Friend, how did you get in here without wedding
clothes?' the king asked him. But the man said nothing. Then the king told
the servants, 'Tie him up hand and foot, and throw him outside in the dark.
There he will cry and gnash his teeth.'"

And Jesus concluded, "Many are invited, but few are chosen."

The Pharisees went off and made a plan to trap Jesus with questions. Then
they sent to him some of their disciples and some members of Herod's party.
"Teacher," they said, "we know that you tell the truth. You teach the truth
about God's will for people, without worrying about what others think,

because you pay no attention to anyone's status. Tell us, then, what do you think? Is it against our Law to pay taxes to the Roman Emperor, or not?"

Jesus, however, was aware of their evil plan, and so he said, "You hypocrites! Why are you trying to trap me? Show me the coin for paying the tax!"

They brought him the coin, and he asked them, "Whose face and name are these?"

"The Emperor's," they answered.

So Jesus said to them, "Well, then, pay to the Emperor what belongs to the Emperor, and pay to God what belongs to God."

When they heard this, they were amazed; and they left him and went away.

That same day some Sadducees came to Jesus and claimed that people will not rise from death. "Teacher," they said, "Moses said that if a man who has no children dies, his brother must marry the widow so that they can have children who will be considered the dead man's children. Now, there were seven brothers who used to live here. The oldest got married and died without having children, so he left his widow to his brother. The same thing happened to the second brother, to the third, and finally to all seven. Last of all, the woman died. Now, on the day when the dead rise to life, whose wife will she be? All of them had married her."

Jesus answered them, "How wrong you are! It is because you don't know the Scriptures or God's power. For when the dead rise to life, they will be like the angels in heaven and will not marry. Now, as for the dead rising to life: haven't you ever read what God has told you? He said, 'I am the God of Abraham, the God of Isaac, and the God of Jacob.' He is the God of the living, not of the dead."

When the crowds heard this, they were amazed at his teaching.

When the Pharisees heard that Jesus had silenced the Sadducees, they came together, and one of them, a teacher of the Law, tried to trap him with a question. "Teacher," he asked, "which is the greatest commandment in the Law?"

Jesus answered, "'Love the Lord your God with all your heart, with all your soul, and with all your mind.' This is the greatest and the most important commandment. The second most important commandment is like it: 'Love your neighbor as you love yourself.' The whole Law of Moses and the teachings of the prophets depend on these two commandments."

When some Pharisees gathered together, Jesus asked them, "What do you think about the Messiah? Whose descendant is he?"

"He is David's descendant," they answered.

Jesus asked, "Why, then, did the Spirit inspire David to call him 'Lord'? David said, 'The Lord said to my Lord: Sit here at my right side until I put your enemies under your feet.' If, then, David called him 'Lord,' how can the Messiah be David's descendant?"

No one was able to give Jesus any answer, and from that day on no one dared to ask him any more questions. (Matthew 22:1–46)

Then Jesus spoke to the crowds and to his disciples. "The teachers of the Law and the Pharisees are the authorized interpreters of Moses' Law. So you must obey and follow everything they tell you to do; do not, however, imitate their actions, because they don't practice what they preach. They tie onto people's backs loads that are heavy and hard to carry, yet they aren't willing even to lift a finger to help them carry those loads. They do everything so that people will see them. Look at the straps with scripture verses on them which they wear on their foreheads and arms, and notice how large they are! Notice also how long are the tassels on their cloaks! They love the best places at feasts and the reserved seats in the synagogues; they love to be greeted with respect in the marketplaces and to have people call them 'Teacher.' You must not be called 'Teacher,' because you are all equal and have only one Teacher. And you must not call anyone here on earth 'Father,' because you have only the one Father in heaven. Nor should you be called 'Leader,' because your one and only leader is the Messiah."

"The greatest one among you must be your servant. Whoever makes himself great will be humbled, and whoever humbles himself will be made great." (Matthew 23:1–12)

# Reflections and Questions

## About the Reading

The Temple in Jerusalem was the most sacred place for the people of Israel, but over time many exploited it for their own profit. Jesus reacted forcefully.

Even visitors that came from Greece wanted to see Jesus. He proclaimed that he will be glorified for all of us. He is the Light that came to illuminate the world. His call to us is to believe in him as the one sent by the Father.

The meaning of the parable of the father with two sons is clear now. The one who initially said yes didn't do what the father wanted; the one who initially said no did do it. What is important for Jesus is doing the will of the Father rather than being concerned about a particular external religious act.

## Let's Meditate

God has a mission for each of us.

- Have you considered that Jesus might react against you if you use religion as a social pretext to gain status or to enrich yourself?
- We are called to prayer. Do you listen to the voice of Jesus frequently and talk with him? What are the changes and challenges he brings to you?
- He who hears the words of Jesus but does not act on them does not accept his message. It makes sense that a person who does not truly believe Jesus will find it difficult to do as he says. How does your belief, or lack of belief, affect your ability to follow Jesus' teaching?
- In the parable of the father with two sons, one finally obeys him and the other does not. With which son do you most closely identify? Can you talk with Jesus about this?
- A royal wedding feast is described from another perspective. How do you understand the point about not being dressed appropriately for the wedding? In what ways do our attitudes, thoughts, feelings, and actions become our daily clothing?

## Ask God

Take some time for quiet reflection. In your own words, ask God to show you, through this Gospel reading, a clear path to the calling he has revealed to you.

## Think about the Main Idea

Look for the phrase in the reading that most catches your attention, and repeat it to yourself several times. You might also write it in a journal so that you can revisit it and think about it again.

## Create an Action Plan

Reading the Bible and praying with it can move us to change.

- How can this reading help you understand your calling better?
- What concrete action can you take to bring your prayer and meditation into daily life?

## Discussion Questions

1. Why would the tax collectors and prostitutes, two groups who were despised in Jesus' day, be quicker to respond to Jesus than the religious rulers of his time? What could that mean for you and the people you know?

2. Jesus avoids the religious leaders' trap by teaching that Caesar (the emperor) has a legitimate claim on their lives, as does God. But Jesus never equates the two. In fact, Jesus' own life shows that obedience to God is more important than anything else. Do you feel any tension between obeying both your government and God right now, and if so, what do you think Jesus wants you to do?

3. Jesus proclaims that the two most important commandments are to love God and to love your neighbors. Why are these two the most important? How are you living out these two commands currently? What would it look like for you to love God or love your neighbor?

## 16

# Talking about the Future

As Jesus sat near the Temple treasury, he watched the people as they dropped in their money. Many rich men dropped in a lot of money; then a poor widow came along and dropped in two little copper coins, worth about a penny. He called his disciples together and said to them, "I tell you that this poor widow put more in the offering box than all the others. For the others put in what they had to spare of their riches; but she, poor as she is, put in all she had—she gave all she had to live on." (Mark 12:41–44)

As Jesus was leaving the Temple, one of his disciples said, "Look, Teacher! What wonderful stones and buildings!"

Jesus answered, "You see these great buildings? Not a single stone here will be left in its place; every one of them will be thrown down."

Jesus was sitting on the Mount of Olives, across from the Temple, when Peter, James, John, and Andrew came to him in private. "Tell us when this will be," they said, "and tell us what will happen to show that the time has come for all these things to take place."

Jesus said to them, "Watch out, and don't let anyone fool you. Many men, claiming to speak for me, will come and say, 'I am he!' and they will fool many people. And don't be troubled when you hear the noise of battles close by and news of battles far away. Such things must happen, but they do not mean that the end has come. Countries will fight each other; kingdoms will attack one another. There will be earthquakes everywhere, and there will be famines. These things are like the first pains of childbirth.

"You yourselves must watch out. You will be arrested and taken to court. You will be beaten in the synagogues; you will stand before rulers and kings for my sake to tell them the Good News. But before the end comes, the gospel must be preached to all peoples. And when you are arrested and taken to court, do not worry ahead of time about what you are going to say; when the time comes, say whatever is then given to you. For the words you speak will not be yours; they will come from the Holy Spirit. Men will hand over their own brothers to be put to death, and fathers will do the same to their children. Children will turn against their parents and have them put to death. Everyone will hate you because of me. But whoever holds out to the end will be saved. (Mark 13:1–13)

"When you see Jerusalem surrounded by armies, then you will know that it will soon be destroyed. Then those who are in Judea must run away to the hills; those who are in the city must leave, and those who are out in the country must not go into the city. For those will be 'The Days of Punishment,' to make come true all that the Scriptures say. How terrible it will be in those days for women who are pregnant and for mothers with little babies! Terrible distress will come upon this land, and God's punishment will fall on this people. Some will be killed by the sword, and others will be taken as prisoners to all countries; and the heathen will trample over Jerusalem until their time is up.

"There will be strange things happening to the sun, the moon, and the stars. On earth whole countries will be in despair, afraid of the roar of the sea and the raging tides. People will faint from fear as they wait for what is coming over the whole earth, for the powers in space will be driven from their courses. Then the Son of Man will appear, coming in a cloud with great power and glory. When these things begin to happen, stand up and raise your heads, because your salvation is near."

Then Jesus told them this parable: "Think of the fig tree and all the other trees. When you see their leaves beginning to appear, you know that summer is near. In the same way, when you see these things happening, you will know that the Kingdom of God is about to come.

"Remember that all these things will take place before the people now living have all died. Heaven and earth will pass away, but my words will never pass away.

"Be careful not to let yourselves become occupied with too much feasting and drinking and with the worries of this life, or that Day may suddenly catch you like a trap. For it will come upon all people everywhere on earth. Be on watch and pray always that you will have the strength to go safely through all those things that will happen and to stand before the Son of Man. (Luke 21:20–36)

"Be ready for whatever comes, dressed for action and with your lamps lit, like servants who are waiting for their master to come back from a wedding feast. When he comes and knocks, they will open the door for him at once. How happy are those servants whose master finds them awake and ready when he returns! I tell you, he will take off his coat, have them sit down, and will wait on them. How happy they are if he finds them ready, even if he should come at midnight or even later! And you can be sure that if the owner of a house knew the time when the thief would come, he would not let the thief break into his house. And you, too, must be ready, because the Son of Man will come at an hour when you are not expecting him."

Peter said, "Lord, does this parable apply to us, or do you mean it for everyone?"

The Lord answered, "Who, then, is the faithful and wise servant? He is the one that his master will put in charge, to run the household and give the other servants their share of the food at the proper time. How happy that servant is if his master finds him doing this when he comes home! Indeed, I tell you, the master will put that servant in charge of all his property. But if that servant says to himself that his master is taking a long time to come back and if he begins to beat the other servants, both the men and the women, and eats and drinks and gets drunk, then the master will come back one day when the servant does not expect him and at a time he does not know. The master will cut him in pieces and make him share the fate of the disobedient.

"The servant who knows what his master wants him to do, but does not get himself ready and do it, will be punished with a heavy whipping. But the servant who does not know what his master wants, and yet does something for which he deserves a whipping, will be punished with a light whipping. Much is required from the person to whom much is given; much more is required from the person to whom much more is given. (Luke 12:35–48)

"At that time the Kingdom of heaven will be like this. Once there were ten young women who took their oil lamps and went out to meet the bridegroom. Five of them were foolish, and the other five were wise. The foolish ones took their lamps but did not take any extra oil with them, while the wise ones took containers full of oil for their lamps. The bridegroom was late in coming, so they began to nod and fall asleep.

"It was already midnight when the cry rang out, 'Here is the bridegroom! Come and meet him!' The ten young women woke up and trimmed their lamps. Then the foolish ones said to the wise ones, 'Let us have some of your oil, because our lamps are going out.' 'No, indeed,' the wise ones answered, 'there is not enough for you and for us. Go to the store and buy some for yourselves.' So the foolish ones went off to buy some oil; and while they were gone, the bridegroom arrived. The five who were ready went in with him to the wedding feast, and the door was closed.

"Later the others arrived. 'Sir, sir! Let us in!' they cried out. 'Certainly not! I don't know you,' the bridegroom answered."

And Jesus concluded, "Watch out, then, because you do not know the day or the hour. (Matthew 25:1–13)

"When the Son of Man comes as King and all the angels with him, he will sit on his royal throne, and the people of all the nations will be gathered before him. Then he will divide them into two groups, just as a shepherd separates the sheep from the goats. He will put the righteous people at his right and the others at his left. Then the King will say to the people on his right, 'Come, you that are blessed by my Father! Come and possess the kingdom which has been prepared for you ever since the creation of the world. I was hungry and you fed me, thirsty and you gave me a drink; I was a stranger and you received me in your homes, naked and you clothed me; I was sick and you took care of me, in prison and you visited me.' The righteous will then answer him, 'When, Lord, did we ever see you hungry and feed you, or thirsty and give you a drink? When did we ever see you a stranger and welcome you in our homes, or naked and clothe you? When did we ever see you sick or in prison, and visit you?' The King will reply, 'I tell you, whenever you did this for one of the least important of these followers of mine, you did it for me!'

"Then he will say to those on his left, 'Away from me, you that are under God's curse! Away to the eternal fire which has been prepared for the Devil and his angels! I was hungry but you would not feed me, thirsty but you would not give me a drink; I was a stranger but you would not welcome me in your homes, naked but you would not clothe me; I was sick and in prison but you would not take care of me.' Then they will answer him, 'When, Lord, did we ever see you hungry or thirsty or a stranger or naked or sick or in prison, and we would not help you?' The King will reply, 'I tell you, whenever you refused to help one of these least important ones, you refused to help me.' These, then, will be sent off to eternal punishment, but the righteous will go to eternal life." (Matthew 25:31–46)

It was now two days before the Festival of Passover and Unleavened Bread. The chief priests and the teachers of the Law were looking for a way to arrest Jesus secretly and put him to death. "We must not do it during the festival," they said, "or the people might riot."

Jesus was in Bethany at the house of Simon, a man who had suffered from a dreaded skin disease. While Jesus was eating, a woman came in with an alabaster jar full of a very expensive perfume made of pure nard. She broke the jar and poured the perfume on Jesus' head. Some of the people there became angry and said to one another, "What was the use of wasting the perfume? It could have been sold for more than three hundred silver coins and the money given to the poor!" And they criticized her harshly.

But Jesus said, "Leave her alone! Why are you bothering her? She has done a fine and beautiful thing for me. You will always have poor people with you, and any time you want to, you can help them. But you will not always have me. She did what she could; she poured perfume on my body to prepare it ahead of time for burial. Now, I assure you that wherever the gospel is preached all over the world, what she has done will be told in memory of her." (Mark 14:1–9)

When the Pharisee who had invited him saw this, he said to himself, "If this man really were a prophet, he would know who this woman is who is touching him; he would know what kind of sinful life she lives!"

Jesus spoke up and said to him, "Simon, I have something to tell you."

"Yes, Teacher," he said, "tell me."

"There were two men who owed money to a moneylender," Jesus began. "One owed him five hundred silver coins, and the other owed him fifty. Neither of them could pay him back, so he canceled the debts of both. Which one, then, will love him more?"

"I suppose," answered Simon, "that it would be the one who was forgiven more."

"You are right," said Jesus. Then he turned to the woman and said to Simon, "Do you see this woman? I came into your home, and you gave me no water for my feet, but she has washed my feet with her tears and dried them with her hair. You did not welcome me with a kiss, but she has not stopped kissing my feet since I came. You provided no olive oil for my head, but she has covered my feet with perfume. I tell you, then, the great love she has shown proves that her many sins have been forgiven. But whoever has been forgiven little shows only a little love."

Then Jesus said to the woman, "Your sins are forgiven."

The others sitting at the table began to say to themselves, "Who is this, who even forgives sins?"

But Jesus said to the woman, "Your faith has saved you; go in peace." (Luke 7:39–50)

A large number of people heard that Jesus was in Bethany, so they went there, not only because of Jesus but also to see Lazarus, whom Jesus had raised from death. So the chief priests made plans to kill Lazarus too, because on his account many Jews were rejecting them and believing in Jesus. (John 12:9–11)

# Reflections and Questions

## About the Reading

Pay attention to what Jesus promised about the future: "Heaven and earth will pass away, but my words will never pass away." Jesus is the eternal Word that the Father speaks to save us. This is why he can affirm our future. It is also striking that he said we shouldn't be preoccupied with the distractions and worries of this life.

Consider the parable of the wise young women who were prepared with oil in their lamps. Similarly, the Judge will say to those who are prepared and served him by serving others, "Come, you that are blessed by my Father!"

This chapter concludes with the mercy of Jesus shown to the woman. He forgives us much, so it is important for us to recognize his love.

## Let's Meditate

God has a mission for each of us.

- Many people are afraid of the end of the world. What could you say to these people, based on this reading?
- Many people today are troubled. Can you identify something that could be troubling you?
- The Lord assured us that he will return. What does it mean to be wise and have oil for your lamp, as in the parable? How can you be prepared? How can you help others to be watchful also?
- Jesus described the things he will ask us in the final judgment. How do you feed the hungry, give drink to the thirsty, welcome strangers, clothe those in need, and visit the sick or imprisoned?
- Do you place your trust in the Lord who is kind and merciful? If you repent, he promised to forgive you. How does your trust in the Lord look and act in daily life?

## Ask God

Take some time for quiet reflection. In your own words, ask God to show you, through this Gospel reading, a clear path to the calling he has revealed to you.

## Think about the Main Idea

Look for the phrase in the reading that most catches your attention, and repeat it to yourself several times. You might also write it in a journal so that you can revisit it and think about it again.

## Create an Action Plan

Reading the Bible and praying with it can move us to change.

- How can this reading help you understand your calling better?
- What concrete action can you take to bring your prayer and meditation into daily life?

## Discussion Questions

1. Why did Jesus praise the poor woman who gave two small copper coins? How would you have felt if you were one of the wealthy people standing nearby?

2. What do you think Jesus meant when he taught, "Much is required from the person to whom much is given; much more is required from the person to whom much more is given"? What have you been given? How are you doing at taking care of what you've been given as you think Jesus would want?

3. Jesus praises those who take care of the most vulnerable people when they are hungry, thirsty, sick, and in prison, because it's actually like taking care of him. Who are the most vulnerable people around you? What would it look like to take care of them as if they were Jesus himself?

# 17

# Betrayed by a Friend

The time was near for the Festival of Unleavened Bread, which is called the Passover. The chief priests and the teachers of the Law were afraid of the people, and so they were trying to find a way of putting Jesus to death secretly.

Then Satan entered into Judas, called Iscariot, who was one of the twelve disciples. So Judas went off and spoke with the chief priests and the officers of the Temple guard about how he could betray Jesus to them. They were pleased and offered to pay him money. Judas agreed to it and started looking for a good chance to hand Jesus over to them without the people knowing about it.

The day came during the Festival of Unleavened Bread when the lambs for the Passover meal were to be killed. Jesus sent Peter and John with these instructions: "Go and get the Passover meal ready for us to eat."

"Where do you want us to get it ready?" they asked him.

He answered, "As you go into the city, a man carrying a jar of water will meet you. Follow him into the house that he enters, and say to the owner of the house: 'The Teacher says to you, Where is the room where my disciples and I will eat the Passover meal?' He will show you a large furnished room upstairs, where you will get everything ready."

They went off and found everything just as Jesus had told them, and they prepared the Passover meal.

When the hour came, Jesus took his place at the table with the apostles. He said to them, "I have wanted so much to eat this Passover meal with you before I suffer! For I tell you, I will never eat it until it is given its full mean-ing in the Kingdom of God." (Luke 22:1–16)

Jesus knew that the hour had come for him to leave this world and go to the Father. He had always loved those in the world who were his own, and he loved them to the very end.

Jesus and his disciples were at supper. The Devil had already put into the heart of Judas, the son of Simon Iscariot, the thought of betraying Jesus. Jesus knew that the Father had given him complete power; he knew that he had come from God and was going to God. So he rose from the table, took off his outer garment, and tied a towel around his waist. Then he poured some water into a washbasin and began to wash the disciples' feet and dry them with the towel around his waist. He came to Simon Peter, who said to him, "Are you going to wash my feet, Lord?"

Jesus answered him, "You do not understand now what I am doing, but you will understand later."

Peter declared, "Never at any time will you wash my feet!"

"If I do not wash your feet," Jesus answered, "you will no longer be my disciple."

Simon Peter answered, "Lord, do not wash only my feet, then! Wash my hands and head, too!"

Jesus said, "Those who have taken a bath are completely clean and do not have to wash themselves, except for their feet. All of you are clean—all except one." (Jesus already knew who was going to betray him; that is why he said, "All of you, except one, are clean.")

After Jesus had washed their feet, he put his outer garment back on and returned to his place at the table. "Do you understand what I have just done to you?" he asked. "You call me Teacher and Lord, and it is right that you do so, because that is what I am. I, your Lord and Teacher, have just washed your feet. You, then, should wash one another's feet. I have set an example for you, so that you will do just what I have done for you. I am telling you the truth: no slaves are greater than their master, and no messengers are greater than the one who sent them. Now that you know this truth, how happy you will be if you put it into practice!

"I am not talking about all of you; I know those I have chosen. But the scripture must come true that says, 'The man who shared my food turned against me.' I tell you this now before it happens, so that when it does happen, you will believe that 'I Am Who I Am.' I am telling you the truth: whoever receives anyone I send receives me also; and whoever receives me receives him who sent me." (John 13:1–20)

Then Jesus took a cup, gave thanks to God, and said, "Take this and share it among yourselves. I tell you that from now on I will not drink this wine until the Kingdom of God comes."

Then he took a piece of bread, gave thanks to God, broke it, and gave it to them, saying, "This is my body, which is given for you. Do this in memory of me." In the same way, he gave them the cup after the supper, saying, "This cup is God's new covenant sealed with my blood, which is poured out for you." (Luke 22:17–20)

After Jesus had said this, he was deeply troubled and declared openly, "I am telling you the truth: one of you is going to betray me."

The disciples looked at one another, completely puzzled about whom he meant. One of the disciples, [John] the one whom Jesus loved, was sitting next to Jesus. Simon Peter motioned to him and said, "Ask him whom he is talking about."

So that disciple moved closer to Jesus' side and asked, "Who is it, Lord?"

Jesus answered, "I will dip some bread in the sauce and give it to him; he is the man." So he took a piece of bread, dipped it, and gave it to Judas, the son of Simon Iscariot. As soon as Judas took the bread, Satan entered into him. Jesus said to him, "Hurry and do what you must!" None of the others at the table understood why Jesus said this to him. Since Judas was in charge of the money bag, some of the disciples thought that Jesus had told him to go and buy what they needed for the festival, or to give something to the poor.

Judas accepted the bread and went out at once. It was night.

After Judas had left, Jesus said, "Now the Son of Man's glory is revealed; now God's glory is revealed through him. And if God's glory is revealed through him, then God will reveal the glory of the Son of Man in himself, and he will do so at once. My children, I shall not be with you very much longer. You will look for me; but I tell you now what I told the Jewish authorities, 'You cannot go where I am going.' And now I give you a new commandment: love one another. As I have loved you, so you must love one another. If you have love for one another, then everyone will know that you are my disciples." (John 13:21–35)

Then they sang a hymn and went out to the Mount of Olives. Jesus said to them, "This very night all of you will run away and leave me, for the scripture says, 'God will kill the shepherd, and the sheep of the flock will be scattered.' But after I am raised to life, I will go to Galilee ahead of you."

Peter spoke up and said to Jesus, "I will never leave you, even though all the rest do!"

Jesus said to Peter, "I tell you that before the rooster crows tonight, you will say three times that you do not know me."

Peter answered, "I will never say that, even if I have to die with you!"

And all the other disciples said the same thing. (Matthew 26:30–35)

Then Jesus asked his disciples, "When I sent you out that time without purse, bag, or shoes, did you lack anything?"

"Not a thing," they answered.

"But now," Jesus said, "whoever has a purse or a bag must take it; and whoever does not have a sword must sell his coat and buy one. For I tell you that the scripture which says, 'He shared the fate of criminals,' must come true about me, because what was written about me is coming true."

The disciples said, "Look! Here are two swords, Lord!"

"That is enough!" he replied. (Luke 22:35–38)

"Do not be worried and upset," Jesus told them. "Believe in God and believe also in me. There are many rooms in my Father's house, and I am going to prepare a place for you. I would not tell you this if it were not so. And after I go and prepare a place for you, I will come back and take you to myself, so that you will be where I am. You know the way that leads to the place where I am going."

Thomas said to him, "Lord, we do not know where you are going; so how can we know the way to get there?"

Jesus answered him, "I am the way, the truth, and the life; no one goes to the Father except by me. Now that you have known me," he said to them, "you will know my Father also, and from now on you do know him and you have seen him."

Philip said to him, "Lord, show us the Father; that is all we need."

Jesus answered, "For a long time I have been with you all; yet you do not know me, Philip? Whoever has seen me has seen the Father. Why, then, do you say, 'Show us the Father'? Do you not believe, Philip , that I am in the Father and the Father is in me? The words that I have spoken to you," Jesus said to his disciples, "do not come from me. The Father, who remains in me, does his own work. Believe me when I say that I am in the Father and the Father is in me. If not, believe because of the things I do. I am telling you the truth: those who believe in me will do what I do—yes, they will do even greater things, because I am going to the Father. And I will do whatever you ask for in my name, so that the Father's glory will be shown through the Son. If you ask me for anything in my name, I will do it.

"If you love me, you will obey my commandments. I will ask the Father, and he will give you another Helper, who will stay with you forever. He is the Spirit, who reveals the truth about God. The world cannot receive him, because it cannot see him or know him. But you know him, because he remains with you and is in you.

"When I go, you will not be left all alone; I will come back to you. In a little while the world will see me no more, but you will see me; and because I live, you also will live. When that day comes, you will know that I am in my Father and that you are in me, just as I am in you.

"Those who accept my commandments and obey them are the ones who love me. My Father will love those who love me; I too will love them and reveal myself to them."

Judas (not Judas Iscariot) said, "Lord, how can it be that you will reveal yourself to us and not to the world?"

Jesus answered him, "Those who love me will obey my teaching. My Father will love them, and my Father and I will come to them and live with them. Those who do not love me do not obey my teaching. And the teaching you have heard is not mine, but comes from the Father, who sent me.

"I have told you this while I am still with you. The Helper, the Holy Spirit, whom the Father will send in my name, will teach you everything and make you remember all that I have told you.

"Peace is what I leave with you; it is my own peace that I give you. I do not give it as the world does. Do not be worried and upset; do not be afraid. You heard me say to you, 'I am leaving, but I will come back to you.' If you loved me, you would be glad that I am going to the Father; for he is greater than I. I have told you this now before it all happens, so that when it does happen, you will believe. I cannot talk with you much longer, because the ruler of this world is coming. He has no power over me, but the world must know that I love the Father; that is why I do everything as he commands me. (John 14:1–31)

"I am the real vine, and my Father is the gardener. He breaks off every branch in me that does not bear fruit, and he prunes every branch that does bear fruit, so that it will be clean and bear more fruit. You have been made clean already by the teaching I have given you. Remain united to me, and I will remain united to you. A branch cannot bear fruit by itself; it can do so only if it remains in the vine. In the same way you cannot bear fruit unless you remain in me.

"I am the vine, and you are the branches. Those who remain in me, and I in them, will bear much fruit; for you can do nothing without me. Those who do not remain in me are thrown out like a branch and dry up; such branches are gathered up and thrown into the fire, where they are burned. If you remain in me and my words remain in you, then you will ask for anything you wish, and you shall have it. My Father's glory is shown by your bearing much fruit; and in this way you become my disciples. I love you just as the Father loves me; remain in my love. If you obey my commands, you will remain in my love, just as I have obeyed my Father's commands and remain in his love.

"I have told you this so that my joy may be in you and that your joy may be complete. My commandment is this: love one another, just as I love you. The greatest love you can have for your friends is to give your life for them. And you are my friends if you do what I command you. I do not call you servants any longer, because servants do not know what their master is doing. Instead, I call you friends, because I have told you everything I heard from my Father. You did not choose me; I chose you and appointed you to go and bear much fruit, the kind of fruit that endures. And so the Father will give you whatever you ask of him in my name. This, then, is what I command you: love one another.

"If the world hates you, just remember that it has hated me first. If you belonged to the world, then the world would love you as its own. But I chose you from this world, and you do not belong to it; that is why the world hates you. Remember what I told you: 'Slaves are not greater than their master.' If people persecuted me, they will persecute you too; if they obeyed my teaching, they will obey yours too. But they will do all this to you because you are mine; for they do not know the one who sent me. They would not have been guilty of sin if I had not come and spoken to them; as it is, they no longer have any excuse for their sin. Whoever hates me hates my Father also. They would not have been guilty of sin if I had not done among them the things that no one else ever did; as it is, they have seen what I did, and they hate both me and my Father. This, however, was bound to happen so that what is written in their Law may come true: 'They hated me for no reason at all.'

"The Helper will come—the Spirit, who reveals the truth about God and who comes from the Father. I will send him to you from the Father, and he will speak about me. And you, too, will speak about me, because you have been with me from the very beginning. (John 15:1–27)

"I have told you this, so that you will not give up your faith. You will be expelled from the synagogues, and the time will come when those who kill you will think that by doing this they are serving God. People will do these things to you because they have not known either the Father or me. But I have told you this, so that when the time comes for them to do these things, you will remember what I told you.

"I did not tell you these things at the beginning, for I was with you. But now I am going to him who sent me, yet none of you asks me where I am going. And now that I have told you, your hearts are full of sadness. But I am telling you the truth: it is better for you that I go away, because if I do not go, the Helper will not come to you. But if I do go away, then I will send him to you. And when he comes, he will prove to the people of the world that they are wrong about sin and about what is right and about God's judgment. They are wrong about sin, because they do not believe in me; they are wrong about what is right, because I am going to the Father and you will not see me any more; and they are wrong about judgment, because the ruler of this world has already been judged.

"I have much more to tell you, but now it would be too much for you to bear. When, however, the Spirit comes, who reveals the truth about God, he will lead you into all the truth. He will not speak on his own authority, but he will speak of what he hears and will tell you of things to come. He will give me glory, because he will take what I say and tell it to you. All that my Father has is mine; that is why I said that the Spirit will take what I give him and tell it to you.

"In a little while you will not see me any more, and then a little while later you will see me."

Some of his disciples asked among themselves, "What does this mean? He tells us that in a little while we will not see him, and then a little while later we will see him; and he also says, 'It is because I am going to the Father.' What does this 'a little while' mean? We don't know what he is talking about!"

Jesus knew that they wanted to question him, so he said to them, "I said, 'In a little while you will not see me, and then a little while later you will see me.' Is this what you are asking about among yourselves? I am telling you the truth: you will cry and weep, but the world will be glad; you will be sad, but your sadness will turn into gladness. When a woman is about to give birth, she is sad because her hour of suffering has come; but when the baby is born, she forgets her suffering, because she is happy that a baby has been born into the world. That is how it is with you: now you are sad, but I will see you again, and your hearts will be filled with gladness, the kind of gladness that no one can take away from you.

"When that day comes, you will not ask me for anything. I am telling you the truth: the Father will give you whatever you ask of him in my name. Until now you have not asked for anything in my name; ask and you will receive, so that your happiness may be complete.

"I have used figures of speech to tell you these things. But the time will come when I will not use figures of speech, but will speak to you plainly about the Father. When that day comes, you will ask him in my name; and I do not say that I will ask him on your behalf, for the Father himself loves you. He loves you because you love me and have believed that I came from God. I did come from the Father, and I came into the world; and now I am leaving the world and going to the Father."

Then his disciples said to him, "Now you are speaking plainly, without using figures of speech. We know now that you know everything; you do not need to have someone ask you questions. This makes us believe that you came from God."

Jesus answered them, "Do you believe now? The time is coming, and is already here, when all of you will be scattered, each of you to your own home, and I will be left all alone. But I am not really alone, because the Father is with me. I have told you this so that you will have peace by being united to me. The world will make you suffer. But be brave! I have defeated the world!" (John 16:1–33)

After Jesus finished saying this, he looked up to heaven and said, "Father, the hour has come. Give glory to your Son, so that the Son may give glory to you. For you gave him authority over all people, so that he might give eternal life to all those you gave him. And eternal life means to know you, the only true God, and to know Jesus Christ, whom you sent. I have shown your glory on earth; I have finished the work you gave me to do. Father! Give me glory in your presence now, the same glory I had with you before the world was made.

"I have made you known to those you gave me out of the world. They belonged to you, and you gave them to me. They have obeyed your word, and now they know that everything you gave me comes from you. I gave them the message that you gave me, and they received it; they know that it is true that I came from you, and they believe that you sent me.

"I pray for them. I do not pray for the world but for those you gave me, for they belong to you. All I have is yours, and all you have is mine; and my glory is shown through them. And now I am coming to you; I am no longer in the world, but they are in the world. Holy Father! Keep them safe by the power of your name, the name you gave me, so that they may be one just as you and I are one. While I was with them, I kept them safe by the power of your name, the name you gave me. I protected them, and not one of them was lost, except the man who was bound to be lost—so that the scripture might come true.

"And now I am coming to you, and I say these things in the world so that they might have my joy in their hearts in all its fullness. I gave them your message, and the world hated them, because they do not belong to the world, just as I do not belong to the world. I do not ask you to take them out of the world, but I do ask you to keep them safe from the Evil One. Just as I do not belong to the world, they do not belong to the world. Dedicate them to yourself by means of the truth; your word is truth. I sent them into the world, just as you sent me into the world. And for their sake I dedicate myself to you, in order that they, too, may be truly dedicated to you.

"I pray not only for them, but also for those who believe in me because of their message. I pray that they may all be one. Father! May they be in us, just as you are in me and I am in you. May they be one, so that the world will believe that you sent me. I gave them the same glory you gave me, so that they may be one, just as you and I are one: I in them and you in me, so that they may be completely one, in order that the world may know that you sent me and that you love them as you love me.

"Father! You have given them to me, and I want them to be with me where I am, so that they may see my glory, the glory you gave me; for you loved me before the world was made. Righteous Father! The world does not know you, but I know you, and these know that you sent me. I made you known to them, and I will continue to do so, in order that the love you have for me may be in them, and so that I also may be in them." (John 17:1–26)

They came to a place called Gethsemane, and Jesus said to his disciples, "Sit here while I pray." He took Peter, James, and John with him. Distress and anguish came over him, and he said to them, "The sorrow in my heart is so great that it almost crushes me. Stay here and keep watch."

He went a little farther on, threw himself on the ground, and prayed that, if possible, he might not have to go through that time of suffering. "Father," he prayed, "my Father! All things are possible for you. Take this cup of suffering away from me. Yet not what I want, but what you want." (Mark 14:32–36)

An angel from heaven appeared to him and strengthened him. In great anguish he prayed even more fervently; his sweat was like drops of blood falling to the ground. (Luke 22:43–44)

Then he returned to the three disciples and found them asleep; and he said to Peter, "How is it that you three were not able to keep watch with me for even one hour? Keep watch and pray that you will not fall into temptation. The spirit is willing, but the flesh is weak."

Once more Jesus went away and prayed, "My Father, if this cup of suffering cannot be taken away unless I drink it, your will be done."

He returned once more and found the disciples asleep; they could not keep their eyes open. Again Jesus left them, went away, and prayed the third time, saying the same words.

Then he returned to the disciples and said, "Are you still sleeping and resting? Look! The hour has come for the Son of Man to be handed over to the power of sinners. Get up, let us go. Look, here is the man who is betraying me!"

Jesus was still speaking when Judas, one of the twelve disciples, arrived. With him was a large crowd armed with swords and clubs sent by the chief priests and the elders. The traitor had given the crowd a signal: "The man I kiss is the one you want. Arrest him!"

Judas went straight to Jesus and said, "Peace be with you, Teacher," and kissed him. (Matthew 26:40–49) But Jesus said, "Judas, is it with a kiss that you betray the Son of Man?"

When the disciples who were with Jesus saw what was going to happen, they asked, "Shall we use our swords, Lord?" And one of them struck the High Priest's slave and cut off his right ear. But Jesus said, "Enough of this!" He touched the man's ear and healed him.

Then Jesus said to the chief priests and the officers of the Temple guard and the elders who had come there to get him, "Did you have to come with swords and clubs, as though I were an outlaw? I was with you in the Temple every day, and you did not try to arrest me. But this is your hour to act, when the power of darkness rules." (Luke 22:48–53)

Then all the disciples left him and ran away. A certain young man [by tradition, Mark] dressed only in a linen cloth, was following Jesus. They tried to arrest him, but he ran away naked, leaving the cloth behind. (Mark 14:50–52)

# Reflections and Questions

## About the Reading

It is surprising that even Jesus, who was so merciful and loving, had friends who suddenly doubted him and betrayed him. Judas, who traded his friendship with Jesus for money, is the example that always comes to mind. But this was also the case with Peter, who didn't stay with Jesus as he promised.

During the Last Supper, Jesus changed roles: he washed the feet of his disciples, which was a slave's job. But he explained that he did it to give an example of humility.

In the end, when they went out to pray together, his closest disciples fell asleep and were not present for Jesus. Then his treacherous friend came back and gave Jesus up with a kiss. But he was no longer the only one; all of Jesus' friends abandoned him and fled.

## Let's Meditate

God has a mission for each of us.

- You may have been betrayed by a person close to you. What is your reaction to reading this episode about Judas betraying Jesus?
- Jesus asks you to give yourself to the service of others. Through what service, and what signs of humility, do you demonstrate that you follow Jesus?
- When has it become most clear to you that Jesus is the Way, the Truth, and the Life to reach God the Father?
- Jesus gave the example of a vine bearing fruit; he is the vine, and we are the branches. How do you stay connected with Jesus so that you can bear spiritual fruit?
- How do you "keep watch" and avoid temptation?

## Ask God

Take some time for quiet reflection. In your own words, ask God to show you, through this Gospel reading, a clear path to the calling he has revealed to you.

## Think about the Main Idea

Look for the phrase in the reading that most catches your attention, and repeat it to yourself several times. You might also write it in a journal so that you can revisit it and think about it again.

## Create an Action Plan

Reading the Bible and praying with it can move us to change.

- How can this reading help you understand your calling better?
- What concrete action can you take to bring your prayer and meditation into daily life?

## Discussion Questions

1. Because the disciples' primary means of transportation was walking, their feet would have been dirty most of the time. What is Jesus communicating when he insists on washing their feet? How could we follow Jesus' example today?

2. Jesus teaches his own followers, "If you have love for one another, then everyone will know that you are my disciples." What messages are communicated to those who do not follow Jesus by the ways that followers of Jesus love—or don't love—one another today? How has God used the love of his followers in your life?

3. Simon Peter is so upset about Jesus' arrest that he pulls out a sword and cuts off the ear of the high priest's slave. But Jesus heals the man's ear. What does that say about how Jesus views those who oppose him? What would it look like to follow Jesus' example when you feel that you want to retaliate against those who hurt you?

# 18

# Facing False Charges

Those who had arrested Jesus took him to the house of Caiaphas, the High Priest, where the teachers of the Law and the elders had gathered together. Peter followed from a distance, as far as the courtyard of the High Priest's house. He went into the courtyard and sat down with the guards to see how it would all come out.

The chief priests and the whole Council tried to find some false evidence against Jesus to put him to death; but they could not find any, even though many people came forward and told lies about him. Finally two men stepped up and said, "This man said, 'I am able to tear down God's Temple and three days later build it back up.'"

The High Priest stood up and said to Jesus, "Have you no answer to give to this accusation against you?" But Jesus kept quiet. Again the High Priest spoke to him, "In the name of the living God I now put you under oath: tell us if you are the Messiah, the Son of God."

Jesus answered him, "So you say. But I tell all of you: from this time on you will see the Son of Man sitting at the right side of the Almighty and coming on the clouds of heaven!"

At this the High Priest tore his clothes and said, "Blasphemy! We don't need any more witnesses! You have just heard his blasphemy! What do you think?"

They answered, "He is guilty and must die."

Then they spat in his face and beat him; and those who slapped him said, "Prophesy for us, Messiah! Guess who hit you!"

Peter was sitting outside in the courtyard when one of the High Priest's servant women came to him and said, "You, too, were with Jesus of Galilee."

But he denied it in front of them all. "I don't know what you are talking about," he answered, and went on out to the entrance of the courtyard. Another servant woman saw him and said to the men there, "He was with Jesus of Nazareth."

Again Peter denied it and answered, "I swear that I don't know that man!"

After a little while the men standing there came to Peter. "Of course you are one of them," they said. "After all, the way you speak gives you away!"

Then Peter said, "I swear that I am telling the truth! May God punish me if I am not! I do not know that man!"

Just then a rooster crowed, and Peter remembered what Jesus had told him: "Before the rooster crows, you will say three times that you do not know me." He went out and wept bitterly. (Matthew 26:57–75)

Early in the morning all the chief priests and the elders made their plans against Jesus to put him to death. They put him in chains and led him off to hand over to Pilate, the Roman governor.

When Judas, the traitor, learned that Jesus had been condemned, he repented and took back the thirty silver coins to the chief priests and the elders. "I have sinned by betraying an innocent man to death!" he said.

"What do we care about that?" they answered. "That is your business!"

Judas threw the coins down in the Temple and left; then he went off and hanged himself.

The chief priests picked up the coins and said, "This is blood money, and it is against our Law to put it in the Temple treasury." After reaching an agreement about it, they used the money to buy Potter's Field, as a cemetery for foreigners. That is why that field is called "Field of Blood" to this very day.

Then what the prophet Jeremiah had said came true: "They took the thirty silver coins, the amount the people of Israel had agreed to pay for him, and used the money to buy the potter's field, as the Lord had commanded me." (Matthew 27:1–10)

Jesus was taken from Caiaphas' house to the governor's palace. The Jewish authorities did not go inside the palace, for they wanted to keep themselves ritually clean, in order to be able to eat the Passover meal. So Pilate went outside to them and asked, "What do you accuse this man of?"

Their answer was, "We would not have brought him to you if he had not committed a crime."

Pilate said to them, "Then you yourselves take him and try him according to your own law."

They replied, "We are not allowed to put anyone to death." (This happened in order to make come true what Jesus had said when he indicated the kind of death he would die.) (John 18:28–32)

They began to accuse him: "We caught this man misleading our people, telling them not to pay taxes to the Emperor and claiming that he himself is the Messiah, a king." (Luke 23:2)

Pilate went back into the palace and called Jesus. "Are you the king of the Jews?" he asked him.

Jesus answered, "Does this question come from you or have others told you about me?"

Pilate replied, "Do you think I am a Jew? It was your own people and the chief priests who handed you over to me. What have you done?"

Jesus said, "My kingdom does not belong to this world; if my kingdom belonged to this world, my followers would fight to keep me from being handed over to the Jewish authorities. No, my kingdom does not belong here!"

So Pilate asked him, "Are you a king, then?"

Jesus answered, "You say that I am a king. I was born and came into the world for this one purpose, to speak about the truth. Whoever belongs to the truth listens to me."

"And what is truth?" Pilate asked.

Then Pilate went back outside to the people and said to them, "I cannot find any reason to condemn him. (John 18:33–38)

But they insisted even more strongly, "With his teaching he is starting a riot among the people all through Judea. He began in Galilee and now has come here."

When Pilate heard this, he asked, "Is this man a Galilean?" When he learned that Jesus was from the region ruled by Herod, he sent him to Herod, who was also in Jerusalem at that time. Herod was very pleased when he saw Jesus, because he had heard about him and had been wanting to see him for a long time. He was hoping to see Jesus perform some miracle. So Herod asked Jesus many questions, but Jesus made no answer. The chief priests and the teachers of the Law stepped forward and made strong accusations against Jesus. Herod and his soldiers made fun of Jesus and treated him with contempt; then they put a fine robe on him and sent him back to Pilate. On that very day Herod and Pilate became friends; before this they had been enemies.

Pilate called together the chief priests, the leaders, and the people, and said to them, "You brought this man to me and said that he was misleading the people. Now, I have examined him here in your presence, and I have not found him guilty of any of the crimes you accuse him of. Nor did Herod find him guilty, for he sent him back to us. There is nothing this man has done to deserve death. So I will have him whipped and let him go." (Luke 23:5–16)

When the chief priests and the Temple guards saw him, they shouted, "Crucify him! Crucify him!"

Pilate said to them, "You take him, then, and crucify him. I find no reason to condemn him."

The crowd answered back, "We have a law that says he ought to die, because he claimed to be the Son of God."

When Pilate heard this, he was even more afraid. He went back into the palace and asked Jesus, "Where do you come from?"

But Jesus did not answer. Pilate said to him, "You will not speak to me? Remember, I have the authority to set you free and also to have you crucified."

Jesus answered, "You have authority over me only because it was given to you by God. So the man who handed me over to you is guilty of a worse sin."

When Pilate heard this, he tried to find a way to set Jesus free. But the crowd shouted back, "If you set him free, that means that you are not the Emperor's friend! Anyone who claims to be a king is a rebel against the Emperor!" (John 19:6–12)

At every Passover Festival the Roman governor was in the habit of setting free any one prisoner the crowd asked for. At that time there was a well-known prisoner named Barabbas. So when the crowd gathered, Pilate asked them, "Which one do you want me to set free for you? Barabbas or Jesus called the Messiah?" He knew very well that the Jewish authorities had handed Jesus over to him because they were jealous.

While Pilate was sitting in the judgment hall, his wife sent him a message: "Have nothing to do with that innocent man, because in a dream last night I suffered much on account of him."

The chief priests and the elders persuaded the crowd to ask Pilate to set Barabbas free and have Jesus put to death. But Pilate asked the crowd, "Which one of these two do you want me to set free for you?"

"Barabbas!" they answered.

"What, then, shall I do with Jesus called the Messiah?" Pilate asked them.

"Crucify him!" they all answered.

But Pilate asked, "What crime has he committed?"

Then they started shouting at the top of their voices: "Crucify him!"

When Pilate saw that it was no use to go on, but that a riot might break out, he took some water, washed his hands in front of the crowd, and said, "I am not responsible for the death of this man! This is your doing!"

The whole crowd answered, "Let the responsibility for his death fall on us and on our children!"

Then Pilate set Barabbas free for them; and after he had Jesus whipped, he handed him over to be crucified. (Matthew 27:15–26)

# Reflections and Questions

### About the Reading

Think about all the people who gathered to conspire against Jesus. Although there was no agreement about the accusations, he was sentenced to death anyway.

It is interesting that those who claimed to be friends of Jesus now denied him, Peter being an example.

The religious leaders resorted to lying to the Roman governor to get him to condemn Jesus. Even the crowd was deceived, and those who had welcomed Jesus as a king a week before now condemned him as a criminal.

### Let's Meditate

God has a mission for each of us.

- On how many occasions have you faced false accusations? How do you respond to the story of Jesus' trial and condemnation?

- When have you been tempted to deny that you were a Christian—or perhaps just fail to mention it—to blend in better or avoid trouble of some sort?

- In what ways are we encouraged to be false with others, even to the point of supporting false accusations? What helps you recognize when a conspiracy is forming against someone, and how do you handle this?

- People in this story made fun of Jesus. Today, we see many forms of abuse, including bullying. What do you do when someone makes fun of your friends or colleagues? Do you stay quiet, or do you get involved to support them? How do you show others that you believe all persons should be respected?

### Ask God

Take some time for quiet reflection. In your own words, ask God to show you, through this Gospel reading, a clear path to the calling he has revealed to you.

## Think about the Main Idea

Look for the phrase in the reading that most catches your attention, and repeat it to yourself several times. You might also write it in a journal so that you can revisit it and think about it again.

## Create an Action Plan

Reading the Bible and praying with it can move us to change.

- How can this reading help you understand your calling better?
- What concrete action can you take to bring your prayer and meditation into daily life?

## Discussion Questions

1. Peter, who had been one of Jesus' closest followers, denies him three times in front of others. Upon realizing what he has done, Peter breaks down and cries. If you encountered Peter when he was crying, what do you think he would say to you? What would you say to him?

2. As Pilate is trying to figure out what to do with Jesus, he asks, "What is truth?" What was the truth about Jesus that Pilate did not understand? How does that truth speak to your life today?

3. Pilate takes a long time before deciding what to do with Jesus and seems very conflicted about whether to give in to the crowd's wishes to crucify Jesus. What would have motivated Pilate to kill Jesus? Why do you think he was hesitant? What would you have done if you were in Pilate's situation?

# 19

# Nailed to a Cross

The soldiers took Jesus inside to the courtyard of the governor's palace and called together the rest of the company. They put a purple robe on Jesus, made a crown out of thorny branches, and put it on his head. Then they began to salute him: "Long live the King of the Jews!" They beat him over the head with a stick, spat on him, fell on their knees, and bowed down to him.

When they had finished making fun of him, they took off the purple robe and put his own clothes back on him. Then they led him out to crucify him.

On the way they met a man named Simon, who was coming into the city from the country, and the soldiers forced him to carry Jesus' cross. (Simon was from Cyrene and was the father of Alexander and Rufus.) (Mark 15:16–21)

A large crowd of people followed him; among them were some women who were weeping and wailing for him. Jesus turned to them and said, "Women of Jerusalem! Don't cry for me, but for yourselves and your children. For the days are coming when people will say, 'How lucky are the women who never had children, who never bore babies, who never nursed them!' That will be the time when people will say to the mountains, 'Fall on us!' and to the hills, 'Hide us!' For if such things as these are done when the wood is green, what will happen when it is dry?"

Two other men, both of them criminals, were also led out to be put to death with Jesus. When they came to the place called "The Skull," they crucified Jesus there, and the two criminals, one on his right and the other on his left.

Jesus said, "Forgive them, Father! They don't know what they are doing."
(Luke 23:27–34)

Pilate wrote a notice and had it put on the cross. "Jesus of Nazareth, the
King of the Jews," is what he wrote. Many people read it, because the place
where Jesus was crucified was not far from the city. The notice was written in
Hebrew, Latin, and Greek. The chief priests said to Pilate, "Do not write 'The
King of the Jews,' but rather, 'This man said, I am the King of the Jews.'"

Pilate answered, "What I have written stays written."

After the soldiers had crucified Jesus, they took his clothes and divided them
into four parts, one part for each soldier. They also took the robe, which was
made of one piece of woven cloth without any seams in it. The soldiers said
to one another, "Let's not tear it; let's throw dice to see who will get it." This
happened in order to make the scripture come true: "They divided my clothes
among themselves and gambled for my robe." And this is what the soldiers
did. (John 19:19–24)

People passing by shook their heads and hurled insults at Jesus: "You were
going to tear down the Temple and build it back up in three days! Save yourself if you are God's Son! Come on down from the cross!"

In the same way the chief priests and the teachers of the Law and the elders
made fun of him: "He saved others, but he cannot save himself! Isn't he the
king of Israel? If he will come down off the cross now, we will believe in him!
He trusts in God and claims to be God's Son. Well, then, let us see if God
wants to save him now!" (Matthew 27:39–43)

One of the criminals hanging there hurled insults at him: "Aren't you the
Messiah? Save yourself and us!"

The other one, however, rebuked him, saying, "Don't you fear God? You
received the same sentence he did. Ours, however, is only right, because we
are getting what we deserve for what we did; but he has done no wrong." And
he said to Jesus, "Remember me, Jesus, when you come as King!"

Jesus said to him, "I promise you that today you will be in Paradise with me." (Luke 23:39–43)

Standing close to Jesus' cross were his mother, his mother's sister, Mary the wife of Clopas, and Mary Magdalene. Jesus saw his mother and [John] the disciple he loved standing there; so he said to his mother, "He is your son." Then he said to the disciple, "She is your mother." From that time the disciple took her to live in his home. (John 19:25–27)

At noon the whole country was covered with darkness, which lasted for three hours. At about three o'clock Jesus cried out with a loud shout, "*Eli, Eli, lema sabachthani?*" which means, "My God, my God, why did you abandon me?" Some of the people standing there heard him and said, "He is calling for Elijah!" (Matthew 27:45–47)

Jesus knew that by now everything had been completed; and in order to make the scripture come true, he said, "I am thirsty."

A bowl was there, full of cheap wine; so a sponge was soaked in the wine, put on a stalk of hyssop, and lifted up to his lips. Jesus drank the wine and said, "It is finished!" (John 19:28–30)

Then Jesus cried out in a loud voice, "Father! In your hands I place my spirit!" He said this and died. (Luke 23:46)

The curtain hanging in the Temple was torn in two from top to bottom. The earth shook, the rocks split apart, the graves broke open, and many of God's people who had died were raised to life. They left the graves, and after Jesus rose from death, they went into the Holy City, where many people saw them.

When the army officer and the soldiers with him who were watching Jesus saw the earthquake and everything else that happened, they were terrified and said, "He really was the Son of God!"

There were many women there, looking on from a distance, who had followed Jesus from Galilee and helped him. Among them were Mary

Magdalene, Mary the mother of James and Joseph, and the wife of Zebedee.
(Matthew 27:51–56)

The Jewish authorities asked Pilate to allow them to break the legs of the men who had been crucified, and to take the bodies down from the crosses. They requested this because it was Friday, and they did not want the bodies to stay on the crosses on the Sabbath, since the coming Sabbath was especially holy.

So the soldiers went and broke the legs of the first man and then of the other man who had been crucified with Jesus. But when they came to Jesus, they saw that he was already dead, so they did not break his legs. One of the soldiers, however, plunged his spear into Jesus' side, and at once blood and water poured out. (The one who saw this happen has spoken of it, so that you also may believe—what he said is true, and he knows that he speaks the truth.) This was done to make the scripture come true: "Not one of his bones will be broken." And there is another scripture that says, "People will look at him whom they pierced."

After this, Joseph, who was from the town of Arimathea, asked Pilate if he could take Jesus' body. (Joseph was a follower of Jesus, but in secret, because he was afraid of the Jewish authorities.) Pilate told him he could have the body, so Joseph went and took it away. Nicodemus, who at first had gone to see Jesus at night, went with Joseph, taking with him about one hundred pounds of spices, a mixture of myrrh and aloes. (John 19:31–39) Joseph took the body, wrapped it in a new linen sheet, and placed it in his own tomb, which he had just recently dug out of solid rock. Then he rolled a large stone across the entrance to the tomb and went away. Mary Magdalene and the other Mary were sitting there, facing the tomb.

The next day, which was a Sabbath, the chief priests and the Pharisees met with Pilate and said, "Sir, we remember that while that liar was still alive he said, 'I will be raised to life three days later.' Give orders, then, for his tomb to be carefully guarded until the third day, so that his disciples will not be able to go and steal the body, and then tell the people that he was raised from death. This last lie would be even worse than the first one."

"Take a guard," Pilate told them; "go and make the tomb as secure as you can."

So they left and made the tomb secure by putting a seal on the stone and leaving the guard on watch. (Matthew 27:59–66)

# Reflections and Questions

## About the Reading

It is notable that a just man, one who has not committed any crime, is condemned anyway. Jesus is forced to carry his cross until he can do it no longer; then the soldiers make a passerby carry it for him. It is important to highlight from these readings how the sacred Scriptures of the Old Testament are fulfilled by Jesus. Thus it is clear that he is the Messiah, and he suffered this most difficult experience to save humankind.

Even as Jesus is being nailed to the cross, he has words of encouragement for others. He prays a psalm.

After Jesus dies, two of his disciples, who had followed him in secret, come to take his body. The religious leaders are concerned, and they ask for his tomb to be guarded.

## Let's Meditate

God has a mission for each of us.

- Today many people suffer from the unjust dealings of others. What is your Christian response to the suffering and oppression you see around you?

- Jesus forgave his executioners. How do you treat those who mistreat you? Do you also know how to forgive others? Are you willing to ask for Jesus' help in learning how to forgive?

- The soldiers took Jesus' clothes. What do you do when you see the powerful taking from the poor? Are you willing to object? How do you act when it happens at your school or workplace?

- Jesus recited the beginning of Psalm 22, which starts with abandonment but culminates in salvation. Have you ever felt abandoned by God? Could you express that in prayer and listen to what the Lord wants to tell you?

- How do you relate to those who followed Jesus secretly? Has that happened to you?

**Ask God**

Take some time for quiet reflection. In your own words, ask God to show you, through this Gospel reading, a clear path to the calling he has revealed to you.

**Think about the Main Idea**

Look for the phrase in the reading that most catches your attention, and repeat it to yourself several times. You might also write it in a journal so that you can revisit it and think about it again.

**Create an Action Plan**

Reading the Bible and praying with it can move us to change.

- How can this reading help you understand your calling better?
- What concrete action can you take to bring your prayer and meditation into daily life?

**Discussion Questions**

1. As Jesus is being nailed to a cross, he says, "Forgive them, Father! They don't know what they are doing!" What does that tell you about Jesus' view of forgiveness? How does that make you feel about the forgiveness that Jesus offers you and others?

2. One of the criminals being crucified alongside Jesus joins in mocking Jesus, while the other asks Jesus, "Remember me, Jesus, when you come as King." Jesus replies to the latter, "I promise you that today you will be in Paradise with me." What could Jesus mean by this?

3. When the Roman commander sees how Jesus dies, he proclaims, "He really was the Son of God!" What aspect of Jesus' death do you think led him to that conclusion? What would it take for you to agree with the Roman commander that Jesus is the Son of God?

# 20

# Back from the Dead

After the Sabbath was over, Mary Magdalene, Mary the mother of James, and Salome bought spices to go and anoint the body of Jesus. Very early on Sunday morning, at sunrise, they went to the tomb.

On the way they said to one another, "Who will roll away the stone for us from the entrance to the tomb?" (It was a very large stone.) Then they looked up and saw that the stone had already been rolled back. So they entered the tomb, where they saw a young man sitting at the right, wearing a white robe—and they were alarmed.

"Don't be alarmed," he said. "I know you are looking for Jesus of Nazareth, who was crucified. He is not here—he has been raised! Look, here is the place where he was placed. (Mark 16:1–6) Remember what he said to you while he was in Galilee: 'The Son of Man must be handed over to sinners, be crucified, and three days later rise to life.'"

Then the women remembered his words, returned from the tomb, and told all these things to the eleven disciples and all the rest. The women were Mary Magdalene, Joanna, and Mary the mother of James; they and the other women with them told these things to the apostles. But the apostles thought that what the women said was nonsense, and they did not believe them. (Luke 24:6–11)

Then Peter and the other disciple went to the tomb. The two of them were running, but the other disciple ran faster than Peter and reached the tomb first. He bent over and saw the linen cloths, but he did not go in. Behind him came Simon Peter, and he went straight into the tomb. He saw the linen cloths lying there and the cloth which had been around Jesus' head. It was not lying with the linen cloths but was rolled up by itself. Then the other disciple, who had reached the tomb first, also went in; he saw and believed. (They still did not understand the scripture which said that he must rise from death.) Then the disciples went back home.

Mary stood crying outside the tomb. While she was still crying, she bent over and looked in the tomb and saw two angels there dressed in white, sitting where the body of Jesus had been, one at the head and the other at the feet. "Woman, why are you crying?" they asked her.

She answered, "They have taken my Lord away, and I do not know where they have put him!"

Then she turned around and saw Jesus standing there; but she did not know that it was Jesus. "Woman, why are you crying?" Jesus asked her. "Who is it that you are looking for?"

She thought he was the gardener, so she said to him, "If you took him away, sir, tell me where you have put him, and I will go and get him."

Jesus said to her, "Mary!"

She turned toward him and said in Hebrew, "Rabboni!" (This means "Teacher.")

"Do not hold on to me," Jesus told her, "because I have not yet gone back up to the Father. But go to my brothers and tell them that I am returning to him who is my Father and their Father, my God and their God."

So Mary Magdalene went and told the disciples that she had seen the Lord and related to them what he had told her. (John 20:3–18)

While the women went on their way, some of the soldiers guarding the tomb went back to the city and told the chief priests everything that had happened. The chief priests met with the elders and made their plan; they gave a large sum of money to the soldiers and said, "You are to say that his disciples came during the night and stole his body while you were asleep. And if the Governor should hear of this, we will convince him that you are innocent, and you will have nothing to worry about."

The guards took the money and did what they were told to do. And so that is the report spread around by the Jews to this very day. (Matthew 28:11–15)

On that same day two of Jesus' followers were going to a village named Emmaus, about seven miles from Jerusalem, and they were talking to each other about all the things that had happened. As they talked and discussed, Jesus himself drew near and walked along with them; they saw him, but somehow did not recognize him. Jesus said to them, "What are you talking about to each other, as you walk along?"

They stood still, with sad faces. One of them, named Cleopas, asked him, "Are you the only visitor in Jerusalem who doesn't know the things that have been happening there these last few days?"

"What things?" he asked.

"The things that happened to Jesus of Nazareth," they answered. "This man was a prophet and was considered by God and by all the people to be powerful in everything he said and did. Our chief priests and rulers handed him over to be sentenced to death, and he was crucified. And we had hoped that he would be the one who was going to set Israel free! Besides all that, this is now the third day since it happened. Some of the women of our group surprised us; they went at dawn to the tomb, but could not find his body. They came back saying they had seen a vision of angels who told them that he is alive. Some of our group went to the tomb and found it exactly as the women had said, but they did not see him."

Then Jesus said to them, "How foolish you are, how slow you are to believe everything the prophets said! Was it not necessary for the Messiah to suffer these things and then to enter his glory?" And Jesus explained to them what was said about himself in all the Scriptures, beginning with the books of Moses and the writings of all the prophets.

As they came near the village to which they were going, Jesus acted as if he were going farther; but they held him back, saying, "Stay with us; the day is almost over and it is getting dark." So he went in to stay with them. He sat down to eat with them, took the bread, and said the blessing; then he broke the bread and gave it to them. Then their eyes were opened and they recognized him, but he disappeared from their sight. They said to each other, "Wasn't it like a fire burning in us when he talked to us on the road and explained the Scriptures to us?"

They got up at once and went back to Jerusalem, where they found the eleven disciples gathered together with the others and saying, "The Lord is risen indeed! He has appeared to Simon!"

The two then explained to them what had happened on the road, and how they had recognized the Lord when he broke the bread.

While the two were telling them this, suddenly the Lord himself stood among them and said to them, "Peace be with you."

They were terrified, thinking that they were seeing a ghost. But he said to them, "Why are you alarmed? Why are these doubts coming up in your minds? Look at my hands and my feet, and see that it is I myself. Feel me, and you will know, for a ghost doesn't have flesh and bones, as you can see I have."

He said this and showed them his hands and his feet. They still could not believe, they were so full of joy and wonder; so he asked them, "Do you have anything here to eat?" They gave him a piece of cooked fish, which he took and ate in their presence. (Luke 24:13–43)

After saying this, he showed them his hands and his side. The disciples were filled with joy at seeing the Lord. Jesus said to them again, "Peace be with you. As the Father sent me, so I send you." Then he breathed on them and said, "Receive the Holy Spirit. If you forgive people's sins, they are forgiven; if you do not forgive them, they are not forgiven."

One of the twelve disciples, Thomas (called the Twin), was not with them when Jesus came. So the other disciples told him, "We have seen the Lord!"

Thomas said to them, "Unless I see the scars of the nails in his hands and put my finger on those scars and my hand in his side, I will not believe."

A week later the disciples were together again indoors, and Thomas was with them. The doors were locked, but Jesus came and stood among them and said, "Peace be with you." Then he said to Thomas, "Put your finger here, and look at my hands; then reach out your hand and put it in my side. Stop your doubting, and believe!"

Thomas answered him, "My Lord and my God!"

Jesus said to him, "Do you believe because you see me? How happy are those who believe without seeing me!" (John 20:20–29)

# Reflections and Questions

## About the Reading

The loyal disciples of Jesus were devastated because of his crucifixion and death. They went to the grave expecting to find a dead body, but he was not there. The text says that one disciple "saw and believed." However, Jesus declared later, "Happy are those who believe without seeing me!"

Many of his followers dispersed because they feared what might happen to them. The story of the two who encountered Jesus on the way to Emmaus opens our minds. Jesus himself explained the Scriptures, and they said that it felt like a fire burning in them.

The risen Jesus sent his disciples to announce the Good News, and he breathed the Holy Spirit on them. The recognition of Jesus as the Messiah and Lord made one declare, "My Lord and my God!"

## Let's Meditate

God has a mission for each of us.

- How often would you prefer to worship Jesus on the cross rather than the risen Christ who challenges you and gives you work to do?
- Do you really believe the witnesses of the resurrection? What hinders this belief? Talk with Jesus about this.
- Is the resurrection of Christ primarily a doctrine you believe, or have you encountered the risen Christ? How are the two different?
- What do you think it will take for you to be transformed from a follower to a missionary disciple through a vital encounter with the risen Jesus?
- Do you, like Thomas, need to see in order to believe? Try to imagine Jesus offering to you his wounds to touch and see.

## Ask God

Take some time for quiet reflection. In your own words, ask God to show you, through this Gospel reading, a clear path to the calling he has revealed to you.

## Think about the Main Idea

Look for the phrase in the reading that most catches your attention, and repeat it to yourself several times. You might also write it in a journal so that you can revisit it and think about it again.

## Create an Action Plan

Reading the Bible and praying with it can move us to change.

- How can this reading help you understand your calling better?
- What concrete action can you take to bring your prayer and meditation into daily life?

## Discussion Questions

1. Why would the chief priests bribe the soldiers to say that Jesus' disciples stole his body while they were sleeping? How have that bribe and lie affected how people respond to Jesus since then?

2. As people like Mary Magdalene, Cleopas, and Thomas come face-to-face with the risen Jesus, they have all sorts of emotions, including fear, joy, and amazement. How would you have felt if you had talked with Jesus or put your fingers in his wounds?

# 21

# More to Come

The eleven disciples went to the hill in Galilee where Jesus had told them to go. When they saw him, they worshiped him, even though some of them doubted.

Jesus drew near and said to them, "I have been given all authority in heaven and on earth. Go, then, to all peoples everywhere and make them my disciples: baptize them in the name of the Father, the Son, and the Holy Spirit, and teach them to obey everything I have commanded you. And I will be with you always, to the end of the age." (Matthew 28:16–20)

He said to them, "Go throughout the whole world and preach the gospel to all people. Whoever believes and is baptized will be saved; whoever does not believe will be condemned. Believers will be given the power to perform miracles: they will drive out demons in my name; they will speak in strange tongues; if they pick up snakes or drink any poison, they will not be harmed; they will place their hands on sick people, and these will get well." (Mark 16:15–18)

After this, Jesus appeared once more to his disciples at Lake Tiberias. This is how it happened. Simon Peter, Thomas (called the Twin), Nathanael (the one from Cana in Galilee), the sons of Zebedee, and two other disciples of Jesus were all together. Simon Peter said to the others, "I am going fishing."

"We will come with you," they told him. So they went out in a boat, but all that night they did not catch a thing. As the sun was rising, Jesus stood at the water's edge, but the disciples did not know that it was Jesus. Then he asked them, "Young men, haven't you caught anything?"

"Not a thing," they answered.

He said to them, "Throw your net out on the right side of the boat, and you will catch some." So they threw the net out and could not pull it back in, because they had caught so many fish.

The disciple whom Jesus loved [John] said to Peter, "It is the Lord!" When Peter heard that it was the Lord, he wrapped his outer garment around him (for he had taken his clothes off) and jumped into the water. The other disciples came to shore in the boat, pulling the net full of fish. They were not very far from land, about a hundred yards away. When they stepped ashore, they saw a charcoal fire there with fish on it and some bread. Then Jesus said to them, "Bring some of the fish you have just caught."

Simon Peter went aboard and dragged the net ashore full of big fish, a hundred and fifty-three in all; even though there were so many, still the net did not tear. Jesus said to them, "Come and eat." None of the disciples dared ask him, "Who are you?" because they knew it was the Lord. So Jesus went over, took the bread, and gave it to them; he did the same with the fish.

This, then, was the third time Jesus appeared to the disciples after he was raised from death.

After they had eaten, Jesus said to Simon Peter, "Simon son of John, do you love me more than these others do?"

"Yes, Lord," he answered, "you know that I love you."

Jesus said to him, "Take care of my lambs." A second time Jesus said to him, "Simon son of John, do you love me?"

"Yes, Lord," he answered, "you know that I love you."

Jesus said to him, "Take care of my sheep." A third time Jesus said, "Simon son of John, do you love me?"

Peter became sad because Jesus asked him the third time, "Do you love me?" and so he said to him, "Lord, you know everything; you know that I love you!"

Jesus said to him, "Take care of my sheep. I am telling you the truth: when you were young, you used to get ready and go anywhere you wanted to; but when you are old, you will stretch out your hands and someone else will tie you up and take you where you don't want to go." (In saying this, Jesus was indicating the way in which Peter would die and bring glory to God.) Then Jesus said to him, "Follow me!"

Peter turned around and saw behind him that other disciple, whom Jesus loved—the one who had leaned close to Jesus at the meal and had asked, "Lord, who is going to betray you?" When Peter saw him, he asked Jesus, "Lord, what about this man?"

Jesus answered him, "If I want him to live until I come, what is that to you? Follow me!"

So a report spread among the followers of Jesus that this disciple would not die. But Jesus did not say he would not die; he said, "If I want him to live until I come, what is that to you?"

He is the disciple [John] who spoke of these things, the one who also wrote them down; and we know that what he said is true. (John 21:1–24)

For forty days after his death he appeared to them many times in ways that proved beyond doubt that he was alive. They saw him, and he talked with them about the Kingdom of God. And when they came together, he gave them this order: "Do not leave Jerusalem, but wait for the gift I told you about, the gift my Father promised. John baptized with water, but in a few days you will be baptized with the Holy Spirit."

When the apostles met together with Jesus, they asked him, "Lord, will you at this time give the Kingdom back to Israel?"

Jesus said to them, "The times and occasions are set by my Father's own authority, and it is not for you to know when they will be. But when the Holy Spirit comes upon you, you will be filled with power, and you will be witnesses for me in Jerusalem, in all of Judea and Samaria, and to the ends of the earth." (Acts 1:3–8)

Then he said to them, "These are the very things I told you about while I was still with you: everything written about me in the Law of Moses, the writings of the prophets, and the Psalms had to come true."

Then he opened their minds to understand the Scriptures, and said to them, "This is what is written: the Messiah must suffer and must rise from death three days later, and in his name the message about repentance and the forgiveness of sins must be preached to all nations, beginning in Jerusalem. You are witnesses of these things. And I myself will send upon you what my Father has promised. But you must wait in the city until the power from above comes down upon you."

Then he led them out of the city as far as Bethany, where he raised his hands and blessed them. As he was blessing them, he departed from them and was taken up into heaven. (Luke 24:44–51)

They still had their eyes fixed on the sky as he went away, when two men dressed in white suddenly stood beside them and said, "Galileans, why are you standing there looking up at the sky? This Jesus, who was taken from you into heaven, will come back in the same way that you saw him go to heaven." (Acts 1:10–11)

They worshiped him and went back into Jerusalem, filled with great joy, and spent all their time in the Temple giving thanks to God. (Luke 24:52–53)

In his disciples' presence Jesus performed many other miracles which are not written down in this book. But these have been written in order that you may believe that Jesus is the Messiah, the Son of God, and that through your faith in him you may have life. (John 20:30–31)

# Reflections and Questions

### About the Reading

Pay attention to the imperative: "Go, then, to all peoples everywhere and make them my disciples." It is a command from Jesus; he promises, "Whoever believes and is baptized will be saved."

Jesus asks, "Do you love me more than these?" Jesus refers to the new opportunities and choices that his resurrection brings us.

Jesus promises a baptism with the Holy Spirit, who gives us the power to be his witnesses.

The two angels in white ask, "Why are you standing there looking up at the sky?" Jesus will return!

### Let's Meditate

God has a mission for each of us.

- Now, at the end of these readings about the life of Jesus, what do you believe about him, and why?
- In your life now, what would be the equivalent of Jesus saying, "throw your net out on the right side of the boat"?
- What mission does Jesus give you in sending you to preach the Good News?
- Have you asked God for the gift of the Holy Spirit to be his witness?
- Believing in Jesus involves not just looking to heaven but also bringing others to an encounter with the risen Lord. Where do you see the Holy Spirit leading you in this mission?

### Ask God

Take some time for quiet reflection. In your own words, ask God to show you, through this Gospel reading, a clear path to the calling he has revealed to you.

## Think about the Main Idea

Look for the phrase in the reading that most catches your attention, and repeat it to yourself several times. You might also write it in a journal so that you can revisit it and think about it again.

## Create an Action Plan

Reading the Bible and praying with it can move us to change.

- How can this reading help you understand your calling better?
- What concrete action can you take to bring your prayer and meditation into daily life?

## Discussion Questions

1. Just prior to Jesus' death, Peter denies Jesus three times, and now Jesus asks Peter three times if he loves him. What point do you think Jesus is trying to make by intentionally posing this question to Peter three times? How do you think Peter feels after this encounter with Jesus?

2. Jesus promises that the Holy Spirit will empower his followers to be witnesses in Jerusalem (their own city), Judea (their region), Samaria (the neighboring region), and in all the earth. How might Jesus want you to spread the Good News of his resurrection with those closest to you, with others you know, and throughout the entire world?

3. The last sentences summarize the hope that the story of Jesus brings to us: that what is written will help you "believe that Jesus is the Messiah, the Son of God, and that through your faith in him you may have life." Do you believe that Jesus is the Messiah? If not, what questions about Jesus still linger for you? If so, how can you experience more of the "life" that comes from belonging to him?

# Glossary

**Abraham** lived about four thousand years ago. He is the ancestor of both the Jewish and Arabic people. Three of the world's major religions—Judaism, Islam, and Christianity—come from his descendants. You can learn more about Abraham in the Old Testament of the Bible (Genesis 12—25).

**apostle** is a special messenger or representative. The twelve disciples of Jesus, and other leaders of the early church, were called apostles.

**crucifixion** is a slow and painful death the Romans used to execute rebels. A person was nailed to a wooden cross with heavy iron nails through the wrists and heel bones. The victim was forced to push down on the nails to be able to breathe. The legs were sometimes broken to make the victim suffocate sooner.

**Daniel** was a prophet who lived during the Jewish captivity in Babylon in the sixth century BC. He became famous for his skill in interpreting dreams and visions.

**David** was a shepherd boy who became a great Jewish king about three thousand years ago. He became famous for killing the giant Goliath (1 Samuel 17). Prophets said that the Messiah would come from the royal family line of David. Both of Jesus' parents descended from King David, but Jesus also claimed to be God's Son.

**demons** are generally regarded as some form of evil, supernatural spirits. In Jesus' time, demons were believed to be responsible for many illnesses. Jesus cast out demons and healed diseases. He spoke to demons directly; sometimes they spoke back.

**destruction of the Temple** happened as Jesus predicted. About forty years after his death, a revolt of the Jews against Roman rule ended with the Romans demolishing the temple and dispersing the Jewish people. For two thousand years the Jews did not have a national homeland again until the country of Israel was established in 1948.

**disciple** means a learner or follower. Jesus choose twelve of his many followers to be his close group of disciples. Some of these twelve, like Simon/Peter or Matthew/Levi have more than one name in the Gospels.

**divorce** of a wife by her husband was allowed by some of the religious leaders for any reason. However, a wife was not permitted to divorce her husband, even if he was unfaithful to her. Women had few rights and were treated like property, but Jesus treated them with respect. He preached about the spiritual significance of a man and woman joining in marriage.

**Elijah** was an important Jewish prophet who lived about 900 years before Jesus. Many Jewish people believed that Elijah would return to prepare the way for the Messiah. Jesus recalled how Elijah miraculously produced food for a starving widow and brought her son back to life (1 Kings 17:8–24).

**Elisha** was Elijah's successor. Jesus told of how Elisha healed Naaman, the commander of a foreign army, from a skin disease (2 Kings 5:1–27).

**family ancestors of Jesus** are listed in the Gospels of Matthew (1:1–17) and Luke (3:23–38). Matthew recorded the family of Jesus through his legal father, Joseph. Many Bible scholars think that Luke recorded the family line of Jesus through his mother Mary—by custom, the name of her husband, Joseph, replaced her name in the family line.

**Festival of Shelters** celebrates the end of harvest. During this feast, people lived in shelters made of branches to remind them of the shelters used by their ancestors as they traveled the desert with Moses.

**food laws** were based on the animals, fish, and birds prohibited in the Law of Moses (Leviticus 11:1–47 and Deuteronomy 14:1–21). The Jewish people had strict rules about what food was considered to be clean, or kosher (a Hebrew word meaning "proper").

**God's name** was claimed by Jesus. The religious leaders became angry when Jesus said, "I AM," because this referred to the holy name God used when he spoke to Moses from a burning bush (Exodus 3:1–15). The Hebrew name is translated as "Yahweh" or "Jehovah" in English.

**Hanukkah** (Festival of the Dedication of the Temple) celebrates the rededication of the temple during the second century BC after the Jewish people rebelled against a Greek king who defiled the temple.

**Herod** became known as Herod the Great because of his grand building projects, including rebuilding the temple in Jerusalem. The Romans appointed him as the king of the Jews in 37 BC, and he ruled for 33 years. After he died, his son Herod Antipas ruled the region of Galilee where Jesus lived.

**Hosanna** comes from a Hebrew expression meaning "save us." The people of Israel used this expression to appeal to their kings for help. It later became an exclamation of praise and honor to God. The people shouted this blessing to Jesus.

**Isaiah** was a major Jewish prophet who lived when the Assyrians captured the ten northern tribes of Israel in 722 BC. Tradition says that he was sawed in half for speaking out against evil.

**Israel** was the name God gave to Jacob—the son of Isaac and grandson of Abraham (Genesis 32:28). The twelve tribes of the nation of Israel were named after Jacob's sons.

**Jeremiah** was a major Jewish prophet who lived when the Babylonians destroyed Jerusalem and exiled the Jewish people in 586 BC. He tried to persuade the Jewish people to repent so God would not punish them for their sins.

**Jesus** comes from the Greek translation of the name *Joshua*. It means "the Lord saves."

**John the Baptist** used baptism (a ritual washing) as a sign that a person had turned away from sin and received God's forgiveness. He told people who had been baptized to change their behavior.

**John** the disciple sometimes referred to himself in his Gospel as "the disciple Jesus loved." He also identified himself both as an eyewitness and one who wrote these things down (John 21:24–25).

**Jonah** was a prophet who tried to run away from God. Sailors threw him over the side of a ship during a wild storm, and he was swallowed by a huge fish sent by God. After three days, the fish spat him up alive onto dry land (Jonah 1—2).

**Lake Galilee** is an inland lake in northern Israel, where Jesus lived for a time nearby. In the Gospels, it is also called the Sea of Galilee, Lake Tiberias, or Lake Gennesaret. The lake is known for sudden storms with violent winds.

**Law of Moses** composes the first five books of the Bible. It is also known as the Jewish Torah. The Law gave instructions about how to obey God and respect other people. Tradition says Moses wrote these books.

**Levites** were assistants to the temple priests. The priests were from the family line of Aaron, who was Moses' brother and the first high priest of Israel.

**Lot** was a nephew of Abraham who lived in the evil city of Sodom. Lot and his family fled when God destroyed this city, but Lot's wife hesitated and was turned into a pillar of salt (Genesis 19:15–29).

**manger** is a feeding box for animals. A stable, cave, or the bottom part of a house were used to shelter farm animals. So Jesus may have been born among the animals.

**manna** was the food God provided to the people of Israel when they wandered in the desert for forty years. Each night white flakes of food fell from the sky (Exodus 16:1–36). Many people of Jesus' time believed that God would again provide manna when the Messiah arrived.

**Messiah** is a Hebrew term that means "the anointed." The title "Christ" comes from the Greek translation of the term. At the time of Jesus' death the Jewish people had been ruled by the Romans for about one hundred years. They were waiting for a Messiah who would come to rule God's kingdom. Many hoped Jesus would free them from Roman occupation. Instead, Jesus preached about the reign of God in the hearts and lives of his followers.

**moneychangers** provided the temple currency. Moneychangers and animal merchants set up their stalls in the area intended for Gentile worshipers. The temple authorities shared in the profits at the people's expense.

**Moses** was a great leader who led the people of Israel out from slavery in Egypt about 3,500 years ago. The people complained as he led them through the desert, so God sent poisonous snakes to punish them. When they asked Moses to help them, God told him to make a bronze snake and lift it up on a pole. The people survived if they looked at it when they were bitten (Numbers 21:6–9). Jesus said he also would be "lifted up" (on a cross) to save people. Today, the symbol of a snake on a pole is used by many medical organizations.

**Noah** built an ark to save his family and animals from a great flood. God brought this flood to punish humans because they had become so evil (Genesis 6—8).

**Passover Feast** is a Jewish festival that celebrates the escape of Israel from slavery in Egypt. God "passed over" the people's homes, sparing them, whereas the eldest son of every Egyptian family died (Exodus 11—12).

**Peter** was the name Jesus gave to his disciple Simon. The name means "a rock" in the Aramaic language that Jesus spoke. The Gospels refer to him by either name and sometimes by both.

**Pharisees** were one of the main groups of Jewish religious leaders in the time of Jesus. The Pharisees were experts in the Law and the prophets.

**Pilate** was appointed to be the governor of Judea and Samaria in AD 26. Pilate had to put down several revolts by the Jewish people while he was the governor.

**prophets** delivered messages from God to the people. These messages were often about future events. Jesus quoted the prophets and said that he had come to fulfill their message. You can find the Old Testament references for these quotations in many Bibles.

**Queen of Sheba** came from the region that is now Yemen to visit King Solomon. In the Gospels she is also called the Queen of the South. She praised God when she saw how much he had blessed Solomon (1 Kings 10:1–13).

**ritual washing** involved washing hands or other parts of the body in a certain way (also called "ablution"). The Pharisees taught people to perform the ritual to purify themselves. Devout Jews performed a ritual washing seven times a day.

**Sabbath** is a holy day set aside by God to be a day of rest (Exodus 20:8–11). The Pharisees made up many extra laws for the Sabbath day, including prohibiting carrying loads, picking wheat, or helping the sick. Christians began to observe the Sabbath on the first day of the week—the day of Jesus' resurrection.

**sacrifice** was a ritual way for people to be forgiven for their sins. The priests offered several sacrifices every day in the temple in Jerusalem. The sacrifices stopped when the Romans destroyed the temple in AD 70.

**Sadducees** were the upper class of the priests and one of the factions of Jewish leaders. They accepted only the Law of Moses and did not believe in resurrection of the dead.

**Samaritans** were a mixed race of people descended from the Jews and foreigners that the Assyrians resettled in Northern Israel. The Samaritans and Jewish people generally despised each other. It was very unusual for a Jewish man even to talk to a Samaritan woman. But Jesus treated the Samaritan woman he met at a well with respect and kindness.

**Sanhedrin** was the Jewish council of elders that acted as Israel's high court.

**Satan** is the name of the devil—the leader of spiritual forces of evil. He is also called Beelzebul in the Gospels.

**shepherds** kept sheep at night in a cave or pen made of stones and branches to protect them from thieves or wild animals. The shepherd usually slept in the entrance to guard his flock. The prophet Ezekiel described the Messiah as the shepherd of people.

**Sodom and Gomorrah** were ancient cities that were known for the wickedness of their people. God destroyed these cities by fire as a punishment (Genesis 19:24–25).

**Solomon** was the son of King David. He was famous for his wisdom and wealth.

**Son of Man** is the title that Jesus often used for himself. It came from a vision of the Messiah described by the Jewish prophet Daniel. He saw God give the Son of Man supreme authority and an everlasting kingdom (Daniel 7:13–14).

**tax collectors** were Jews working for the Roman authorities. They were despised as traitors who enriched themselves at the expense of their own people. Often they stole by collecting more than the taxes due.

**Temple curtain** covered the entrance to the Most Holy Place, which was the inner sanctuary where God appeared to the High Priest. The High Priest could go beyond the curtain only once a year to seek forgiveness for the people's sins. The curtain was torn open when Jesus died on the cross.

**Ten Commandments** were laws given by God to Moses (Exodus 20, Deuteronomy 5). Jesus quoted from the Ten Commandments and explained their true meaning. He talked about the importance of our attitudes as well as our actions.

**Theophilus** may have been a Roman or a Greek official. Luke dedicated his Gospel to Theophilus, whose name means "one who loves God."

**Tiberius** was the Roman emperor at the time of Jesus. He lived from AD 14 to 37.

**Tyre and Sidon** were two ancient cities that God punished because of the people's sin (Ezekiel 28).

**whipping** or scourging of prisoners by the Romans could be fatal. The whip was made of several strips of leather with pieces of sharp bone and metal attached that tore off pieces of flesh.

**Word** is special term for God. John in his Gospel identified Jesus as the Word that existed in the beginning. So the story of Jesus does not start at his birth but at the start of all things.

# References

This chart lists the events of Jesus' life in chronological order and indicates where these events appear in each of the four Gospels.

| | Matthew | Mark | Luke | John | Page |
|---|---|---|---|---|---|
| **Chapter 1** | | | | | |
| God is the eternal Word | | | | 1:1–5 | 1 |
| God becomes a human being | | | | 1:9–18 | 1 |
| Gospel writer's introduction | | 1:1 | 1:1–4 | | 1 |
| Birth of John announced | | | 1:5–25 | | 2 |
| Birth of Jesus announced | | | 1:26–56 | | 3 |
| Birth of John the Baptist | | | 1:57–80 | | 4 |
| **Chapter 2** | | | | | |
| Jesus given his name | 1:18–25 | | | | 9 |
| Birth of Jesus | | | 2:1–20 | | 9 |
| The baby Jesus is blessed | | | 2:21–38 | | 10 |
| Wise Men visit Jesus | 2:1–12 | | | | 11 |
| Jesus' family returns to Nazareth | 2:13–23 | | 2:39–40 | | 12 |
| The boy Jesus at the temple | | | 2:41–52 | | 13 |
| **Chapter 3** | | | | | |
| John the Baptist preaches | 3:1–12 | 1:2–8 | 3:1–18 | 1:6–8 | 17 |
| John baptizes Jesus | 3:13–17 | 1:9–11 | 3:21–23 | | 18 |
| Jesus tempted in the desert | 4:1–11 | 1:12–13 | 4:1–13 | | 19 |
| John talks about who he is | | | | 1:15 | 19 |

| | Matthew | Mark | Luke | John | Page |
|---|---|---|---|---|---|
| Jewish leaders plan to kill Jesus | 12:14–15 | 3:6 | 6:11 | 5:18 | 40 |
| **Chapter 6** | | | | | |
| Crowds come to Jesus | 12:16–21 | 3:7–12 | 6:17–19 | | 45 |
| Jesus chooses the 12 disciples | 10:1–4 | 3:13–19 | 6:12–16 | | 45 |
| Jesus preaches Sermon on the Mount | 5:1–12 | | 6:20–26 | | 46 |
| About being salt and light | 5:13–16 | | 14:34 | | 46 |
| About conflict with others | 5:17–25 | | | | 47 |
| About adultery and divorce | 5:27–32 | | | | 48 |
| About loving our enemies | 5:38–48 | | 6:27–36 | | 48 |
| The Lord's Prayer | 6:6–13 | | 11:1–4 | | 49 |
| About wealth and worry | 6:19–34 | | 12:22–34 | | 50 |
| About judging others | 7:1–6 | | 6:37–42 | | 51 |
| The Golden Rule | 7:12 | | 6:31 | | 51 |
| About false teachers | 7:15–23 | | 6:43–45 | | 52 |
| Parable of wise and foolish builders | 7:24–29 | | 6:46–49 | | 52 |
| **Chapter 7** | | | | | |
| Jesus heals commander's servant | 8:5–13 | | 7:1–10 | | 55 |
| Jesus raises widow's son from dead | | | 7:11–17 | | 55 |
| Jesus talks about John the Baptist | 11:1–19 | | 7:18–35 | | 56 |
| Jesus promises rest for the weary | 11:25–30 | | | | 57 |
| Many women support Jesus | | | 8:1–3 | | 57 |

| | Matthew | Mark | Luke | John | Page |
|---|---|---|---|---|---|
| Jesus accused of using evil powers | 12:22–37 | 3:22–30 | 11:14–28 | | 58 |
| Jesus asked for sign from God | 12:38–45 | | 11:29–32 | | 59 |
| Jesus talks about his true family | 12:46–50 | 3:31–35 | 8:19–21 | | 59 |
| Parable of the seed and soils | 13:1–23 | 4:1–25 | 8:4–18 | | 60 |
| Parables about God's kingdom | 13:24–51 | 4:26–34 | 13:18–21 | | 61 |
| **Chapter 8** | | | | | |
| Jesus calms a storm | 8:23–27 | 4:35–41 | 8:22–25 | | 67 |
| Jesus delivers man from demons | 8:28–34 | 5:1–20 | 8:26–39 | | 67 |
| Jesus brings girl back to life | 9:18–26 | 5:21–43 | 8:40–56 | | 68 |
| Woman touches Jesus' clothes | 9:20–22 | 5:25–34 | 8:43–48 | | 69 |
| Jesus' own townspeople reject him | 13:53–58 | 6:1–6 | | 4:44 | 70 |
| Jesus sends out his disciples | 10:5–16 | 6:7–13 | 9:1–6 | | 71 |
| Jesus warns of persecution | 10:17–33 | | 12:2–12 | | 71 |
| Jesus warns of family strife | 10:34–42 | | 12:49–53 | | 72 |
| Herod kills John the Baptist | 14:1–12 | 6:14–29 | 9:7–9 | | 73 |
| **Chapter 9** | | | | | |
| Jesus feeds 5000 | 14:13–21 | 6:30–44 | 9:10–17 | 6:1–15 | 77 |
| Jesus walks on the lake | 14:22–36 | 6:45–56 | | 6:16–21 | 78 |
| Jesus is "the bread of life" | | | | 6:22–71 | 79 |
| Jesus talks about being "unclean" | 15:1–20 | 7:1–23 | | | 81 |

| | Matthew | Mark | Luke | John | Page |
|---|---|---|---|---|---|
| Canaanite woman shows her faith | 15:21–28 | 7:24–30 | | | 83 |
| Jesus heals deaf and dumb man | 15:29–31 | 7:31–37 | | | 83 |
| Jesus feeds 4000 | 15:32–39 | 8:1–10 | | | 84 |
| Jesus warns about religious leaders | 16:1–12 | 8:11–21 | | | 84 |
| **Chapter 10** | | | | | |
| Jesus heals blind man | | 8:22–26 | | | 89 |
| Peter says Jesus is the Messiah | 16:13–20 | 8:27–30 | 9:18–20 | | 89 |
| Jesus talks about following him | 16:21–28 | 8:31–9:1 | 9:21–27 | | 90 |
| Jesus transfigured with God's glory | 17:1–13 | 9:2–13 | 9:28–36 | | 90 |
| Jesus heals boy with evil spirit | 17:14–21 | 9:14–29 | 9:37–43 | | 91 |
| Jesus talks more about his death | 17:22–23 | 9:30–32 | 9:44–45 | | 92 |
| Coin in a fish's mouth | 17:24–27 | | | | 92 |
| Jesus talks about humility | 18:1–14 | 9:33–50 | 9:46–50 | | 93 |
| Jesus talks about forgiveness | 18:15–35 | | | | 94 |
| **Chapter 11** | | | | | |
| Jesus' brothers don't believe him | | | | 7:1–10 | 99 |
| Jesus talks about following him | 8:18–22 | | 9:51–62 | | 99 |
| Pharisees attempt to arrest Jesus | | | | 7:11–53 | 101 |
| Jesus forgives woman of adultery | | | | 8:1–11 | 102 |
| Jesus is "the light of the world" | | | | 8:12–20 | 103 |

| | Matthew | Mark | Luke | John | Page |
|---|---|---|---|---|---|
| Jesus says he came from heaven | | | | 8:21–30 | 104 |
| Jesus says he was sent by God | | | | 8:31–47 | 104 |
| Jesus claims God's sacred name | | | | 8:48–59 | 106 |
| **Chapter 12** | | | | | |
| Jesus sends out 72 followers | 11:20–24 | | 10:1–24 | | 109 |
| Parable of the Good Samaritan | | | 10:25–37 | | 111 |
| Jesus visits Mary and Martha | | | 10:38–42 | | 111 |
| Jesus condemns religious leaders | 23:13–36 | | 11:37–12:1 | | 112 |
| Warning about wanting wealth | | | 12:13–21 | | 113 |
| Warning about sin and death | | | 13:1–9 | | 113 |
| Jesus heals woman on Sabbath | | | 13:10–17 | | 114 |
| Jesus heals blind man on Sabbath | | | | 9:1–41 | 114 |
| Jesus says he is "the Good Shepherd" | | | | 10:1–18 | 117 |
| Jesus accused of being crazy | | | | 10:19–21 | 118 |
| Jesus says he is "God's Son" | | | | 10:22–42 | 118 |
| **Chapter 13** | | | | | |
| Jesus talks about the narrow way | 8:11–12 | | 13:22–30 | | 123 |
| Jesus grieves over Jerusalem | 23:37–39 | | 13:31–35 | | 123 |

| | Matthew | Mark | Luke | John | Page |
|---|---|---|---|---|---|
| Jesus heals man with swollen body | | | 14:1–6 | | 124 |
| Parables about feasts | | | 14:7–24 | | 124 |
| Jesus talks more about cost | | | 14:25–35 | | 125 |
| Parable of prodigal son | | | 15:11–32 | | 126 |
| Parable of the clever manager | | | 16:1–15 | | 127 |
| Parable of the beggar and the rich man | | | 16:19–31 | | 128 |
| Jesus talks about forgiveness | | | 17:1–10 | | 129 |
| Jesus' friend Lazarus dies | | | | 11:1–16 | 130 |
| Jesus is "the resurrection and life" | | | | 11:17–27 | 131 |
| Jesus raises Lazarus from the dead | | | | 11:28–44 | 132 |
| Jewish leaders plan to kill Jesus | | | | 11:45–54 | 132 |
| **Chapter 14** | | | | | |
| Jesus heals ten men with skin disease | | | 17:11–19 | | 137 |
| Jesus talks about his kingdom | | | 17:20–37 | | 137 |
| Parables about prayer | | | 18:1–14 | | 138 |
| Jesus talks about divorce | 19:1–12 | 10:1–12 | 16:16–18 | | 139 |
| Jesus blesses little children | 19:13–15 | 10:13–16 | 18:15–17 | | 140 |
| Jesus meets rich young man | 19:16–30 | 10:17–31 | 18:18–30 | | 140 |
| Parable of the vineyard workers | 20:1–16 | | | | 141 |
| Jesus predicts his death | 20:17–19 | 10:32–34 | 18:31–34 | | 142 |

| | Matthew | Mark | Luke | John | Page |
|---|---|---|---|---|---|
| Jesus predicts destruction of temple | 24:1–2 | 13:1–2 | 21:5–6 | | 163 |
| Signs of the end of the world | 24:3–22 | 13:3–20 | 21:7–26 | | 164 |
| Jesus' talks about his future return | 24:23–35 | 13:21–32 | 21:27–38 | | 165 |
| Being ready for Jesus' return | 24:36–51 | 13:33–37 | 12:35–48 | | 165 |
| Parable about bridesmaids | 25:1–13 | | | | 166 |
| The final judgment of everyone | 25:31–46 | | | | 166 |
| Woman pours perfume on Jesus | 26:6–13 | 14:3–9 | 7:36–50 | 12:1–11 | 167 |
| **Chapter 17** | | | | | |
| Judas agrees to betray Jesus | 26:1–16 | 14:10–11 | 22:1–6 | | 173 |
| Disciples prepare Passover meal | 26:17–19 | 14:12–16 | 22:7–13 | | 173 |
| Jesus washes disciples' feet | | | | 13:1–17 | 174 |
| Jesus shares the Last Supper | 26:20–30 | 14:17–26 | 22:14–30 | 13:18–32 | 175 |
| Jesus predicts Peter's denial | 26:31–35 | 14:27–31 | 22:31–38 | 13:33–38 | 176 |
| Jesus is the "way, truth and life" | | | | 14:1–14 | 177 |
| Jesus promises to send Holy Spirit | | | | 14:15–31 | 177 |
| Jesus commands us to love one another | | | | 15:1–17 | 179 |
| Jesus talks about persecution | | | | 15:18—16:4 | 179 |
| Jesus is returning to the Father | | | | 16:5–33 | 180 |

| | Matthew | Mark | Luke | John | Page |
|---|---|---|---|---|---|
| Jesus prays for his followers | | | | 17:1–26 | 182 |
| Jesus sweats blood in Gethsemane | 26:36–46 | 14:32–42 | 22:39–46 | 18:1–2 | 183 |
| Jesus is betrayed and arrested | 26:47–56 | 14:43–52 | 22:47–54 | 18:3–12 | 184 |
| **Chapter 18** | | | | | |
| Jesus tried by Jewish council | 26:57–66 | 14:53–64 | 22:54 | 18:13–24 | 189 |
| Guards beat and abuse Jesus | 26:67–68 | 14:65 | 22:63–65 | | 189 |
| Peter denies knowing Jesus | 26:69–75 | 14:66–72 | 22:55–62 | 18:15–27 | 190 |
| Jesus sentenced to die | 27:1–2 | 15:1 | 22:66–71 | | 190 |
| Judas Iscariot hangs himself | 27:3–10 | | | | 190 |
| Jesus tried by Pilate | 27:11–14 | 15:2–5 | 23:1–6 | 18:28–38 | 191 |
| Jesus tried by Herod | | | 23:7–12 | | 192 |
| Pilate hands Jesus over to die | 27:15–26 | 15:6–15 | 23:13–25 | 18:39—19:16 | 193 |
| The soldiers whip Jesus | 27:26 | 15:15 | | 19:1 | 194 |
| **Chapter 19** | | | | | |
| The soldiers mock Jesus | 27:27–31 | 15:16–20 | 23:11 | 19:2–3 | 197 |
| Jesus nailed to a cross | 27:32–44 | 15:21–32 | 23:26–43 | 19:17–27 | 197 |
| Jesus dies on the cross | 27:45–56 | 15:33–41 | 23:44–49 | 19:28–37 | 199 |
| Pilate gives Jesus' body to Joseph of Arimathea | 27:57–61 | 15:42–47 | 23:50–56 | 19:38–42 | 200 |
| Guards seal Jesus' tomb | 27:62–66 | | | | 200 |
| **Chapter 20** | | | | | |
| Jesus rises from the dead | 28:1–7 | 16:1–8 | 24:1–12 | 20:1–10 | 205 |

| | Matthew | Mark | Luke | John | Page |
|---|---|---|---|---|---|
| Jesus appears to Mary Magdalene | 28:8–10 | 16:9–11 | | 20:11–18 | 206 |
| Priests bribe guards to lie | 28:11–15 | | | | 206 |
| Jesus appears on road to Emmaus | | 16:12–13 | 24:13–35 | | 207 |
| Jesus appears to his disciples | | 16:14 | 24:36–43 | 20:19–20 | 208 |
| Jesus appears to Thomas | | | | 20:24–29 | 208 |
| **Chapter 21** | | | | | |
| Jesus commissions his disciples | 28:16–20 | 16:15–18 | 24:44–49 | 20:21–23 | 213 |
| Miraculous catch of fish | | | | 21:1–14 | 213 |
| Jesus encourages Peter | | | | 21:15–22 | 214 |
| Jesus promises power of the Spirit | | | ACTS 1:2–8* | | 215 |
| Jesus ascends to heaven | | 16:19 | 24:50–51 | | 216 |
| Jesus will come back again | | | ACTS 1:9–11* | | 216 |
| The purpose of the Gospels | | | | 20:30–31 | 216 |

*Because The Acts of the Apostles continues the story of Jesus' followers begun in The Gospel according to Luke, the two citations from Acts are included in the "Luke" column.

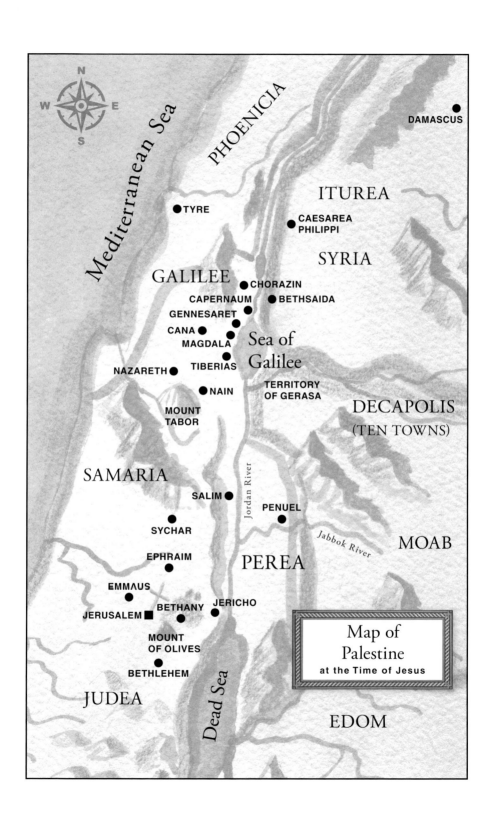

N
W E
S

Mediterranean Sea

PHOENICIA

DAMASCUS

ITUREA

TYRE

CAESAREA
PHILIPPI

SYRIA

GALILEE

CHORAZIN
CAPERNAUM ● BETHSAIDA
GENNESARET
CANA ●
MAGDALA

Sea of
Galilee

TIBERIAS

NAZARETH ●

NAIN

TERRITORY
OF GERASA

DECAPOLIS
(TEN TOWNS)

MOUNT
TABOR

SAMARIA

SALIM

Jordan River

PENUEL

Jabbok River

MOAB

SYCHAR

EPHRAIM

PEREA

EMMAUS

JERICHO

JERUSALEM ■ BETHANY

MOUNT
OF OLIVES

BETHLEHEM

Dead Sea

JUDEA

EDOM

Map of
Palestine
at the Time of Jesus

Saint JOHN PAUL II, World Youth Day, Paris, August 1997.

BENEDICT XVI, World Youth Day, Madrid, August 2011.

FRANCIS, World Youth Day, Krakow, July 2016.